Faith

THE ULTIMATE GUIDE WHAT FAITH IS HOW FAITH WORKS HOW TO GET FAITH HOW TO USE FAITH TO RECEIVE FROM GOD

Jim Kibler

ACKNOWLEDGEMENTS

Mary Kibler, my wife and ministry partner for her suggestions, editing and support.

Jean Johnson, for her suggestions, editing and prayers.

Our Wonderful Church Family for their support and encouragement.

My Prayer Partners, whom I pray with every day.

CONTENTS

INTRODUCTION

I know a little bit about FAITH. Enough to get my prayers answered, as well as the prayers of others. To get sick people healed and to cause THE BLESSING of God to come upon people.

Miracles are routine in my ministry because I know the SECRET KEY to making them happen and having them follow me. I can do what the great healing evangelists did, years ago. I can even use my FAITH to make things happen in my life and in the lives of other people, because I know the "Necessary combination."

I know how to receive from God and I can help others receive what they want or need also.

I know how to develop and increase FAITH, even using short-cuts to quickly grow FAITH.

I know how to remove doubt.

I know how to boost your FAITH.

I know an easy way to receive from God.

It has only taken me 30 years to learn what I now know about FAITH. I estimate that I have spent somewhere in the neighborhood of 20,000 hours studying God's Word or listening to good Word of FAITH teaching. I calculate that if I keep learning at the same rate for the next 300 years, I am going to know a little bit more about FAITH.

FAITH is the most powerful force in the universe. It will cause Almighty God, the Creator of Heaven and Earth, the One who holds the earth, the sun and all of the planets in the palm of His Hand, to do things for you and to move on your behalf.

Have you ever wondered why some people seem to receive from God and some don't? The answer, of course, is always FAITH. Some people have FAITH and some don't. Some have a higher level of FAITH than others.

FAITH is what connects us to the promises of God, which have already been provided for us by the redemptive work of Jesus. I have heard people say that FAITH connects people to the power of God and they are right.

You are where you are at, in every area of your life, because of where your level of FAITH is at, in each area.

You are not bound by your surroundings, who you are, where you came from or anything else. FAITH will overcome all of those things.

FAITH will actually change the course of nature in your life. It will change the natural progression of things and make everything work out to your advantage.

According to 1 John 5:4, FAITH gives us the victory that allows us to overcome the natural world system of sin, sickness, disease, poverty, stress, fear and a hard life.

FAITH Allows us to live **above** all situations and circumstances, not under them.

Abraham is the father of FAITH and Kenneth Hagin is the father of the WORD OF FAITH MOVEMENT. The movement, which teaches that Jesus suffered and died on the cross to give us eternal salvation, and included in His redemption, was health and an abundant good life.

I did not have a personal relationship with Brother Hagin, as many others did, but Mary and I were BLESSED to have met him and to sit in his classes at Bible College. I even got saved reading the back of one of his little books, while working at a used car lot in Tomahawk, Wisconsin. He presented both of us with our diplomas when we graduated from Bible College. That was a great honor.

This book is a result of absorbing his teachings as well as that of Kenneth Copeland, Charles Capps, Keith Moore, Doug Jones, Fred Price, Creflo Dollar, Billye Brim, Leroy Thompson, John Osteen and others. And also, the revelation of God's Word that has been given to me.

Everywhere in the Bible, where you see the words **FAITH** or **BELIEVE,** you can actually substitute the words **EXPECT or EXPECTATION** in their place. The words are interchangeable. Where used in this book, they are capitalized because of their importance. Just for fun, go through the New Testament and change the words around from FAITH and BELIEVE to EXPECT OR EXPECTATION. It will make it easier for you to understand FAITH.

ALL ABOUT RESULTS

This book is all about using FAITH to get results. It doesn't do any good to teach people about FAITH unless they also learn how to use it to get what they want or need from God, so that is also emphasized in this book.

The most important thing I have learned about FAITH is **how simple this really is** and that is what I am sharing in this book. I intend for this book to take you to a much higher level of FAITH, so that you can live the abundant, healthy, stress free, happy life that Jesus came to provide for us.

After you read this book, you will know as much about FAITH as I do, maybe more. You will then be able to use your FAITH to do what I do, to have what I have and to be a BLESSING in the Kingdom of God. How simple is that?

If you think this book is amazing, tell everyone you know about it.

Warning: Possible side effects of reading this book.

- May cause extreme excitement.
- Your finances may increase.
- Your health may improve.
- Your debt may be reduced or go away.
- You may experience miracles in your life.
- You may begin getting your prayers answered on a regular basis.
- Generational curses may be broken from your life.
- You may start living a happy stress-free life.

FAITH DEFINED

FAITH FACT: FAITH is the most powerful force in your life.

FAITH FACT: FAITH is available to everyone.

FAITH FACT: FAITH must always be based on God's Word.

FAITH is the most important subject in the Bible because FAITH gives us access to all the promises of God, including salvation.

FAITH is simply BELIEVING that <u>God is able</u> and EXPECTING that <u>God will</u> perform what He has promised in His Word.

Hebrews 11:1 Now faith is the substance of things hoped for, the evidence of things not seen.

In the King James Bible there are major mistranslations in this verse. Please look these words up for yourself in the Greek concordance.

The word <u>substance</u> in this verse should have been translated ASSURANCE or CONFIDENCE.

The word <u>hoped</u> should have been translated EXPECT or EXPECTATION.

The word <u>evidence</u> means proof beyond a reasonable DOUBT.

Now FAITH is the CONFIDENT ASSURANCE of things EXPECTED, the CERTAINTY OR PROOF BEYOND ANY DOUBT of things not yet seen.

FAITH is EXPECTING to receive something that you cannot yet see, or EXPECTING something to happen, without any doubt in your heart whatsoever.

FAITH is to BELIEVE, or to take God at His Word, to put absolute trust in Him for your every want or need. In the Old Testament, the word TRUST means FAITH.

A person with FAITH in God is a person who quite simply just BELIEVES what God said, that His Word is true, without exception and without any doubt.

Proverbs 3:5 Trust in the Lord with all of your heart and do not depend on your own understanding.

FAITH does not try to figure out how or when something will happen. It just EXPECTS that it will happen.

FAITH is BELIEVING God's Word. When you do, it will be accounted to you for righteousness, which is right standing with God.

FAITH knows the outcome of any circumstance or situation.

FAITH is a spiritual force that can be used to effect change.

FAITH overrides nature and time.

FAITH trumps all evil.

TRUE FAITH

2 Timothy 1:5 I remember the unfeigned, (GENUINE OR TRUE) FAITH that is in your heart, which dwelt first in the heart of your grandmother Lois, and in the heart of your mother Eunice and I am sure, is in your heart also.

TRUE FAITH is always in a person's heart.

TRUE FAITH is based only on the Word of God and absolutely nothing else. This is the Abraham type of FAITH.

TRUE FAITH always gets results.

A person with TRUE FAITH is willing to bet their life on the Word of God, just as the disciples did, after they had seen the risen Christ.

People who have TRUE FAITH depend on God alone. They actually have FAITH that God provides all of their needs and according to Jeremiah 17:7-8, those people are BLESSED and are like a tree planted by the waters and will not even notice when, or if, a famine comes.

TRUE FAITH refuses to be denied, once the will of God has been established.

TRUE FAITH absolutely refuses to be defeated.

TRUE FAITH has removed doubt by refusing to consider any and all circumstances.

Ephesians 6:16 TRUE FAITH is the shield that is used to quench ALL the fiery darts of the enemy. Fiery darts are sickness, disease, poverty, fear, stress, anxiety, worry, and the enemy's attempts to discourage you.

Proverbs 4:23 Protect your heart because the issues of life come out of it.

The enemy is always trying to steal God's Word out of your heart. (Mark 4:15) If that happens, your BLESSINGS will stop. David said in **Psalm 119:11 Thy Word have I hid in my heart.** God's Word should be hidden in your heart and protected.

SENSE FAITH

SENSE FAITH is BELIEF based upon the five senses, as well as physical evidence, emotions or feelings. Many times, this type of FAITH is also based on the experiences of other people, both good and bad. It is sometimes called the Thomas type of FAITH. People who say, "I will BELIEVE it when I see it."

John 20:25 Thomas said, unless I see in His hands the print of the nails and put my finger into the hole of the nails and thrust my hand into His side I will not believe.

He had to see before he would BELIEVE, and Jesus said he was FAITHLESS. Then Jesus said "BLESSED are those who have not seen, yet have BELIEVED."

HEAD FAITH

John Wesley referred to this as MENTAL ASSENT. He said this is a substitute for FAITH that looks and sounds so much like TRUE FAITH that few people can tell the difference. I call it HEAD FAITH, just to make it easier to understand, because it actually is FAITH that is in a person's head, not in their heart. Some people call it MENTAL FAITH.

HEAD FAITH can be very dangerous, both to the person who has a head full of FAITH and to people they try to minister to. People with little or no discernment are oftentimes very impressed with these people because of their knowledge of the scriptures, the way they talk, and the confidence they have in themselves. They act and talk like FAITH powerhouses.

The rule of thumb in judging another person's FAITH, is not by what they say, or how they act, but by what is actually going on in their life. If they are sick and broke you can tell that their FAITH is only in their head.

THEY DON'T KNOW WHAT THEY DON'T HAVE

People who have MENTAL FAITH think they have plenty of FAITH. They will question the will of God and make excuses for why they have not yet received. They will try to reason things out, doubt if they are on the right track, hunt for a verse to stand on, and are quick to accept defeat. I have heard many of them say, "God must be teaching me patience."

Many of these people don't know that their FAITH is only in their head. They do not know that they do not have TRUE FAITH and can become very frustrated when trying to receive from God, because they will not admit that their FAITH is not where it needs to be. They BELIEVE they have GREAT FAITH and cannot understand why it is not working for them.

18 INCHES

I heard Neal Syvertson and others say, "Many people will miss Heaven by 18 inches." The distance between the head and the heart. People also miss their healing, financial increase and THE BLESSING by the same distance.

James 1:22 But be doers of the Word and not hearers only.

- A doer of the Word is a person who, when something happens, right away starts relying on and speaking God's Word.

- A hearer only, is a person who when something happens, forgets everything they have heard because their FAITH is in their head and not in their heart.

2 TYPES OF BABY CHRISTIANS

James 3:2 Whoever does not defile themselves with their words is a mature person.

That also means that people who curse themselves with their words, are immature, or what we call, **Baby Christians**. According to Hebrews 5:12 and 1 Corinthians 3:2, they need to be fed milk, not the meat of God's Word.

- **New Babies** This is the first type of baby Christians. These are the people who have just been saved and are very excited by everything that is going on in church and in their new life. They are easy to minister to and receive quickly from God because they do not question anything they hear and usually do not try to reason things out for themselves. They have a child like FAITH.

- **Old Babies** The second type of baby Christians. These are the people who are quick to tell everyone how long they have been saved. They are easy to spot because they do not control the words they say about themselves. They try to impress people with their FAITH but many times are sick and broke themselves. Mary says, "They are like a Shetland Pony who thinks he is a big horse."

KNOWING GOD'S WORD IS NOT ENOUGH

Years ago, when we were still living in Wisconsin, there was a man who knew the Bible backwards and forwards. He could quote chapter and verse on just about any subject. He was quick to jump in and try to minister to anyone who had a problem of any kind. The only problem was the fact that he was sick and very broke himself. I quickly realized that even though he had FAITH, his FAITH was all in his head.

You can always tell how much FAITH a person has by how much they have received from God.

When people want everyone to think they have great FAITH, we have a right to question that and I absolutely do question people's FAITH. I judge a person's FAITH not on what they say, how long they have been saved, or how much of the Bible they have memorized, but only on the results they are getting in their own life. Always remember, if a person is staying sick and broke it is because they have NO FAITH.

Do not let yourself be led down the wrong path, or be ministered to, by people who have no FAITH themselves.

I know another man, quiet, friendly and unassuming. He does not pass himself off as anything special, but in reality, he is a man of GREAT FAITH. He very seldom makes a mistake in business and gives away millions of dollars to support the work of the Lord. He is a wonderful BLESSING to the Kingdom.

I caused quite an uproar on Facebook a couple of years ago when a lady who had been suffering with cancer for years said, "I live by FAITH." I made a comment and said, "If you had FAITH you would be healed by now." Well, you would have thought I insulted Mother Theresa. People went ballistic on me. "How dare you question her faith" they said. Others said "I have known her for years and she is a great woman of FAITH."

I may have been somewhat insensitive, but I also told her we could get her healed through the Power of God. She was not interested in that. She said she was "Just going to go by the Bible." It's a shame she does not know what it says about healing.

People like to say, "I am BELIEVING God." I always ask, for what and based on what? Most of the time, these people never receive anything.

When Mary and I arrived at Rhema Bible College, one of the first things I did was to observe Kenneth Hagin, his family and staff to see how they were living and what was going on in their lives. I discovered that they were not only teaching FAITH, but were also people of GREAT FAITH themselves. They teach God's Word and they live by God's Word. Observing that for myself, said more to me about Brother Hagin, his family and the staff at Rhema than anything anyone could have ever told me. We knew we were in the right place.

I have heard Kenneth Copeland, a man of GREAT FAITH himself, talk about how he used to watch Oral Roberts use his FAITH to make things happen. That was also a man of GREAT FAITH.

Many people know God's Word and even teach FAITH, but how many people do you know who can actually use their FAITH to make things happen?

FEAR

FEAR FACT: FEAR is the opposite of FAITH.

FEAR FACT: Just like FAITH comes by hearing God's Word in your ear, FEAR comes by hearing in your ear, bad words, bad news, words of discouragement, or words from the devil.

Bad words produce FEAR. In Numbers Chapter 13, the children of Israel **listened** to a bad report, which produced FEAR and UNBELIEF in their heart. As a result, except for a few, they all died in the wilderness. Joshua and Caleb refused to FEAR, or to BELIEVE anything, except for what God had said. Eventually, both of them received their inheritance in the promised land, just as God had promised.

People who are in fear have NO FAITH.

GREAT FEAR

2 Timothy 1:7 God has not given us a spirit of FEAR but of power and of love and of a sound mind.

FEAR is an evil spirit that comes upon people and also causes stress, anxiety and depression. This evil spirit is subject to THE NAME OF JESUS.

FEAR is the exact opposite of GREAT FAITH.

Job was very rich and successful, but he worried about his children all the time. His biggest mistake was in giving voice to his FEAR. In Job 1:5 **Job SAID, "Maybe my sons have sinned by cursing God in their hearts."** His FEAR gave the devil access to his life and he lost all that he had including his health.

> **Job 3:25 What I greatly FEARED has come upon me and what I was afraid of has come unto me.**

You cannot be in FAITH and be FEARFUL about something at the same time.

HEART FEAR

HEART FEAR is FEAR that has been spoken by your mouth, heard by your ear and gone down into your spirit. **It will give the devil access to your life**. Read Job chapter 1.

HEAD FEAR is FEAR in your head that will go away if it is not spoken. FEAR in your head will not hurt you **if** you keep your mouth shut!

God's Word drives out FEAR and the more of God's Word that you hear, the less FEAR you will have.

LEVELS OF FAITH

Jesus described 4 levels of FAITH:

Level One: NO FAITH.

> **Mark 4:40 Jesus said unto them, why are you so fearful? How is it that you have NO FAITH?**

NO FAITH = FEAR. People at this level, worry, are depressed, have anxiety and live lives full of stress.

Level Two: LITTLE FAITH.

> **Matthew 16:8 Jesus said unto them, O you of little FAITH, why reason among yourselves, because you have brought no food?**

People with LITTLE FAITH are always trying to reason things out.

> **Proverbs 3:5 Trust in the Lord with all your heart and do not depend on your own understanding.**

Level Three: FAITH.

> **Mark 10:52 Jesus said unto him, go your way, your faith has made you whole.**

People with FAITH are the ones who get healed and receive from God. A person with FAITH, refuses to be denied or defeated.

Level Four: GREAT FAITH

> **Matthew 15:28 Jesus said to her, O woman, great is your FAITH, be it unto you just as you want. Matthew 8:10 Jesus said to them that followed Him, I have not found such GREAT FAITH in all of Israel.**

This is a very small group of people. It is one thing to know about FAITH. It is another thing entirely, to be able to make things happen just by speaking, and that is what people with GREAT FAITH can do. GREAT FAITH speaks the word only, demands and EXPECTS results.

People with NO FAITH receive nothing from God.

People with LITTLE FAITH receive little from God.

People with FAITH receive from God, but many times it is a battle. However, they will always win because they refuse to be defeated.

People with GREAT FAITH receive easily from God and they live an abundant, stress free, happy life in a place of rest.

You can tell where your FAITH is at by how much you receive from God or how much stress, anxiety or fear you have in your life. Take some time to determine your level of FAITH in different areas of your life.

I describe the levels of FAITH this way: Four people with four different levels of FAITH, each in their own boat in the middle of the sea and a storm comes up.

The person with NO FAITH will drown for sure.

The person with LITTLE FAITH might survive, or might drown.

The person with FAITH will survive because they will refuse to drown. They will turn their boat into the storm and fight their way through. They will most definitely survive, but it could be a battle.

The person with GREAT FAITH will speak the Word only, tell the storm to stop in the NAME OF JESUS, and go through on calm seas.

The way you deal with the storms that come up in your life depends on your level of FAITH. In Mark 4:39 Jesus did not fight His way through the storm, He said "Stop, be still."

We had a major life changing crisis in our family a couple of years ago and instead of dealing with it, fighting our way through it and maybe having it change our lives, I just told it to stop in the Name of Jesus. Within three hours everything was back to normal.

Last year we had another crisis involving someone else in our family who is under my spiritual authority. Instead of accepting the situation, I told it to stop in the Name of Jesus and within two days the person was back to normal and getting on with their life.

I deal with storms every day in the lives of my prayer partners with amazing results. I have purposed to never fight my way through another storm, ever!

Do not be deceived by how simple this is.

Everyone has a certain level of FAITH in each area of their lives. In some areas I do have GREAT FAITH, in some areas I do not. I can tell the difference.

Many people try to operate on a higher level of FAITH than they have developed. These same people will die of sickness and disease or go broke standing on FAITH that they do not have.

Operate on the level of FAITH where you are at in each area of your life while increasing your level of FAITH for where you want to be.

THE LAW OF FAITH

FAITH FACT: God will do nothing for anyone without FAITH.

FAITH FACT: There is nothing God will not do for anyone who has FAITH in, or BELIEVES what He said.

> **Romans 3:27 Where does the credit go, to the law of works, no: but to the law of FAITH.**

A law is something that works the same way every time. If God ever made an exception and BLESSED or healed someone apart from FAITH, the law of FAITH would no longer be in effect. The law of FAITH is applied equally and is no respecter of people, situations or circumstances.

FAITH LAW # 1

> **Hebrews 11:6 But without FAITH a person cannot please God.**

What this verse really means is that without FAITH, no person will ever get anything from God. No exceptions!!!

The leader of a very large prayer organization died, sick and broke, because he had NO FAITH. He had been sick, off and on for years, and his family had to ask for contributions to help pay for his memorial service. Because of the law of FAITH, God will never make an exception, even for such a wonderful man as this who had dedicated himself to The Lord's work all his life.

In order to please God, we must BELIEVE what He said and EXPECT things to happen exactly the way He said they will, with no doubt.

FAITH LAW #2

Mark 11:23 Jesus said, whatever you desire when you pray, EXPECT that you will receive it and you will get it.

We must EXPECT that we will receive it **before** we will actually have it.

God will never save anyone, heal anyone, or provide for anyone unless they EXPECT Him to.

God wants three things from us. He wants us to love Him with all of our heart, love each other, and **BELIEVE** what He has said.

FAITH LAW #3

Matthew 9:29 Jesus said to them, be it unto you according to your FAITH.

Everyone is going to receive everything they get from God, **only** according to their FAITH.

All the BLESSINGS of God come to us according to our FAITH.

Romans 5:2 By whom also we have access, by FAITH, into God's Grace.

God's Grace is wonderful, but because of the law of FAITH, we do not even get Grace without FAITH and that includes saving Grace and serving Grace. The amount of Grace we get from God is according to how much we EXPECT, or have FAITH to receive.

FAITH LAW #4

Romans 10:17 FAITH comes by hearing God's Word in your ear.

This is an important aspect of the law of FAITH. You can increase FAITH by reading God's Word but it will come a lot faster if you read it out loud.

FAITH only comes from hearing and then BELIEVING what you heard.

FAITH LAW #5

Galatians 5:6 It doesn't matter who you are, FAITH is made complete by love.

You must have love in your heart for God and for God's people in order for FAITH to work in your life. According to Mark 11:25

FAITH will not work unless you forgive others, no matter what they have done and that takes love.

FAITH LAW #6

Hebrews 10:23 God is FAITHFUL to what He has promised.

You must BELIEVE God will do what He has promised. There is no such thing as failure to receive from God when the law of FAITH is met, no matter the situation or circumstances.

FAITH LAW #7

2 Corinthians 5:7 For we walk by FAITH not by sight.

The foundation for your FAITH must be based on what God said, not what you have seen, what you now see, or the experiences of other people.

THE LAW OF DOUBT

DOUBT FACT: Doubt is the major FAITH blocker.

DOUBT FACT: Doubt will turn GREAT FAITH into LITTLE FAITH.

DOUBT FACT: Doubt always brings fear.

WHEN YOU DOUBT YOU GO WITHOUT

A person who doubts is a person who is **not sure** of something.

Doubt comes from information you have received that is contrary to what you BELIEVE.

People are not born with doubt. It is learned through not being told the truth.

> **James 1:6-7 but let him ask in FAITH with <u>no doubt</u> for he that doubts is like a wave of the sea driven with the wind and tossed. Let not that person think that they shall receive anything of the Lord.**

If you doubt that you are going to get your prayers answered, you will receive nothing from God.

The moment a person asks **why** God has not answered a prayer, or begins to look **for the reason** why they have not received, or **accepts delay**, they are defeated because they are DOUBTING.

The word doubt means uncertainty, lack of conviction or to question. To consider something happening unlikely, or to consider more than one outcome.

When people question God's Word they are doubting God's Word and FAITH will not work for them. People who constantly ask, **when** will God do something and **how** is God going to do it, are expressing doubt.

DOUBT IS A DECISION

John chapter 20 Thomas decided to doubt and not BELIEVE that Jesus had risen from the dead, unless he saw Him and the holes in His hands and side.

In Genesis chapter 3, Eve decided to doubt that God was telling her the truth because she listened when the devil told her she would not die if she ate from the tree of good and evil. Listening to the serpent caused her to doubt that what God had told her was the truth.

Mary Thomas said, "If you are increasing your FAITH to receive something from God, it may not always be a good idea to tell other people." Be careful who you tell, they may fill you with doubt.

Doubt is a tool of the devil to make us lack confidence in God's Word and thus prevent us from possessing the promises of God.

THE BLESSING BLOCKER

Considering circumstances, instead of God's Word, will always bring doubt and fear and will block THE BLESSINGS of God in your life.

Matthew 14:25-31 Peter had GREAT FAITH when he saw Jesus walking on the water and he was told to "Come." But doubt turned Peter's GREAT FAITH into LITTLE FAITH and he sank. What brought on the doubt was when Peter took his eyes off of Jesus and decided to considered the circumstances (the storm). Jesus then ask Peter, "Why did you doubt Me?" FAITH caused Peter to walk on the water, but doubt sunk him.

After Peter sank, he did have FAITH in Jesus to save him and Jesus then reached down His Hand and pulled him up. Peter had reconnected to Jesus by FAITH.

FAITH moved Peter from the natural to the supernatural and doubt took him back to the natural. FAITH took him back again to the supernatural, where Jesus saved him.

HEAD DOUBT AND HEART DOUBT

Doubt that goes through your head will not block your FAITH and cause you to not receive from God, if FAITH is in your heart.

Luke 1:1-22 When Zechariah was told by the angel of the Lord that he and his wife, Elizabeth, would have a son in their old age he doubted. The angel then closed his mouth so he could not continue to speak his doubt, because doubt unspoken is harmless and will not block the plan of God in your life. When doubt comes into your mind, KEEP YOUR MOUTH SHUT, or you will receive nothing from God.

It is natural for thoughts of doubt to go through your head from time to time. However, doubt will not get into your heart unless you speak it out loud. The ear is the gateway to the heart. Don't let words of doubt get into your heart through your ear.

Mark 4:24 Jesus said, "be careful what you hear."

Jesus said in **Mark 11:23 if we do not doubt in our heart we can have what we say.** He did not say anything about doubting in our head.

James 1:5-8 Tells us that when we ask God for wisdom (Or anything else) we are to ask in FAITH, with no doubt as to whether or not we are going to receive it. This passage goes on to say that if we doubt, when we ask God, we will not receive anything from Him because we are unstable in all of our ways.

Romans 4:19-21 Abraham became strong in FAITH when he stopped considering his own body, when he was about a hundred years old, neither the deadness of Sarah's womb.

He got to the point where he refused to consider the circumstances, or anything, other than the promise of God.

Gideon defeated a huge army with only 300 men because he refused to consider anything other than the fact that God told him, "I will save you with 300 men." (Judges Chapter 7:7)

Isaac became very rich during a famine, while surrounded by the enemy because he refused to consider anything other than the fact that God said, "Stay here and I will BLESS you." (Genesis 26:1-14)

Remove all doubt and your FAITH will work every time.

REFUSE TO CONSIDER

The simplest way to remove all doubt and quickly begin to receive from God is to **absolutely refuse to consider** anything other than what God's Word says.

God's Word says I am healed by the stripes of Jesus and I **refuse to consider** any other outcome. I also refuse to even listen to anyone who tries to tell me different.

God's Word says that THE BLESSING OF ABRAHAM is mine and I **refuse to consider** anything that happens with the economy, the government, the banks, my job, or anything else. Nothing else matters but THE BLESSING and I will prosper and live in abundance, no matter what happens around me. How about you?

HOW FAITH COMES

FAITH FACT: FAITH is a gift that only comes by hearing the Word of God.

FAITH FACT: God will not increase your FAITH.

FAITH FACT: What you continually hear, you will eventually BELIEVE.

I think it is safe to say, that the FAITH of Jesus, during the time He was on this earth, was PERFECT in every area of His life. The rest of us however, can increase our FAITH on a daily basis, while looking to Him, as our example.

I try to increase my FAITH at least some, every day.

STEP #1

Romans 12:2 That you may know what the will of God is.

FAITH begins where the will of God is known. You must know it is **God's will** for you to have what you are asking for, or what you want or need.

STEP #2

Romans 4:21 Abraham became fully persuaded that what God had promised, He was able to perform.

You must become **fully persuaded** that God **is able** to deliver on His promises. Most Christians BELIEVE this, but some do not.

STEP #3

Hebrews 11:11 Sarah herself received strength to conceive seed and gave birth to a child when she was past the childbearing age because she decided that God would do what He had promised.

FAITH is EXPECTING that God will do for you what He has promised.

STEP #4

James 1:6 But let a person ask, and EXPECT to get it, without any doubt.

When you get to the point where you **EXPECT to receive** something **without doubting,** God is going to give it to you every time, without fail and without delay.

People are not born with FAITH or beliefs. Faith comes from a decision whether or not to BELIEVE information that you have received.

A child has complete FAITH in the words of his or her parents, until they say something that is not right, or not true, and then that complete FAITH is gone forever.

INCREASING YOUR FAITH

John Thomas, a man in our church, said, "Your now condition is a result of your NOW FAITH." What you have now and what you are accomplishing in your life **now** is a result of how strong your FAITH is **now**. However, you can increase what you have **now** and what you are accomplishing **now**, simply by increasing your FAITH. Do not be deceived by how simple this is.

> **Romans 10: 17 So then Faith comes by hearing the Word of God in your ear.**

This is the main way to get, or to increase your FAITH.

The two easiest ways to **hear** God's Word are to read your Bible out loud, or recite the verses out loud.

Another way that FAITH comes is through good preaching of God's Word. Find good preachers and teachers who have an anointing to increase your FAITH. I always tell people, "If I am not increasing your FAITH, I am wasting your time."

I encourage people to keep listening because you never know if the next time you hear me say something from God's Word, that it might drop down into your heart and change your life.

However, be careful who you listen to. Not all preachers are teaching FAITH. I heard a nationally known, so called "Man of God," tell his listeners, "God may not want to heal you." That man is a FAITH destroyer.

FAITH DOES NOT COME BY PRAYING

Do not pray for FAITH. A lady at a conference said to me, "Pastor Jim, I have spent all day asking God to increase my FAITH." I told her, "You are wasting your time and God's. FAITH comes by hearing God's Word.

YOUR FAITH DOES GROW

2 Thessalonians 1:3 That your FAITH grows exceedingly.

Brother Hagin told us one day in class, that he had reached the point where he could BELIEVE God for a million dollars now, just as easy as he used to BELIEVE God for a hundred dollars. I know that in my own life, my FAITH is much stronger than it was only a few years ago, and it is now much easier for me to receive from God.

MAKE A DECISION

To BELIEVE what God says or not begins with a choice. I decided years ago, that I am going to BELIEVE every Word that is in the Bible, exactly as it is written. Because of that decision there is no way anyone can ever convince me that even one Word in the Bible is not true.

After you hear God's Word, you must also decide whether or not to BELIEVE it.

If anyone says anything that is different than what the Bible says, I will refuse to believe them.

BE CAREFUL WHO YOU LISTEN TO

God told Adam and his wife that they could eat of all the trees in the garden except one, or they would die. They BELIEVED, for a time, what God had said. However, Eve started listening to the devil and put her FAITH in the devil's words instead of God's. I think we all know how that worked out. At some point she decided to BELIEVE what the serpent said.

When a person has access to your ears they have the potential of increasing your FAITH, or changing what you BELIEVE. I am very careful who has access to the flaps on the side of my head.

BECOME EMPOWERED

The minute you admit that you do not have the FAITH for what you want or need, you become empowered to increase your FAITH. The problem is that many people will not admit that they do not have enough FAITH for something.

My personal rule is this: if I am not quickly receiving what I want or need, I will start increasing my FAITH, by hearing and speaking God's Word in that area until I get it. I have heard both Kenneth Copeland and Creflo Dollar talk about doing that and it sure seems to work for them.

THE MEASURE OF FAITH

Romans 12:3 God has given each person His measure (Limited portion) of FAITH.

According to Strong's Exhaustive Concordance, the word measure, used in Romans 12:3 means by implication, a limited portion.

Romans 10:8 The Word is near to your mouth and in your heart, that is the Word of FAITH which we preach.

According to Kenneth Hagin, every saved person has been given a measure of FAITH, that has come from hearing the Word of FAITH. That measure of FAITH will grow and develop according to the amount of God's Word that you listen to.

The measure of FAITH we receive from God by hearing His Word can be increased, but you are the only one who can increase it. When we hear God's Word, He will measure out Faith that will go into our heart. It works the same way for healing, abundance and THE BLESSING. The more of God's Word you hear, the larger the measure of FAITH you are given for what you want or need.

Ephesians 2:8 For by grace are you saved through FAITH, that is not of yourself, it is the gift of God.

FAITH is a gift of God, given to us through hearing His Word. (Romans 10:17)

In Romans 10:8 Paul called the Word he preached, the Word of FAITH, because God's Word will cause FAITH to come into your heart when you hear it.

FAITH FOOD

To keep your body in good shape you must eat right and exercise. You also keep your FAITH in good shape by feeding it the Word of God. Then you exercise it by putting it into practice. The more you feed and exercise it, the stronger it gets, just like your body gets stronger when you exercise it and keep it nourished with the right kind of food.

Matthew 4:4 Man shall not live by bread alone but by every Word that God speaks.

Our FAITH and our spirits are both designed to receive their nourishment by being fed the Word of God, which God Himself has furnished.

CONFESSION

Confession is God's method of increasing FAITH.

Hebrews 10:23 Do not stop confessing your FAITH.

Joshua 1:8 Keep speaking out loud, My Word, during the day and also at night so that you will learn to do what is written in it and then you will become prosperous and have good success.

The reason these verses are in the Bible is because God knows that if you say something enough times, what you BELIEVE in your head will move down into your heart (Spirit) and will cause your FAITH to work for you.

Time spent hearing and speaking God's Word is an investment that will pay off with an increase of what you receive from God.

When you speak God's Word you are giving voice to God's Word and you will hear it in your ear. Because your ear is only 4 inches from your mouth, you are the first person to hear anything that you say. Speaking God's Word over and over will cause FAITH to come because everything you say goes into your ear.

The purpose of speaking God's Word is to increase your FAITH, by you hearing the Word of God over and over again. Remember, your FAITH comes by **you** hearing God's Word.

When you use God's method of increasing your FAITH for what you want or need, there is nothing you cannot have. This is how the most successful people of GREAT FAITH do it. If you will do what they do, you can have what they have.

I decided years ago to do the same thing that they do and if I keep doing it I will someday soon be living and ministering on the same level. Anyone can do the same thing if they are persistent enough.

CONNECTING IN FAITH

Confession is the tool that God has instructed us to use, and it will cause us to connect to God in FAITH, if we keep doing it.

Romans 10:9-10 tells us we must confess with our mouth and BELIEVE in our heart for salvation. Everything else, including healing and THE BLESSING works the same way. You must confess with your mouth until you BELIEVE and then you will have it.

God promised Abraham and his wife, Sarah, a son, but the truth of the matter is that for 24 years, because of their age, they did not BELIEVE that God had the ability to make it happen. He was almost 100 and she was approaching 90.

In order to increase their FAITH, God visited Abraham and changed his name from Abram to Abraham which means, **father of many**. Abraham was then forced to call himself, father of many. Sarah had to call her husband, father of many. Everyone he talked to or did business with had to call him, father of many. Can you imagine how many times a day he must have heard himself called, father of many? God had to get Abraham to confess it and hear it until he BELIEVED it.

> **Romans 4:19 Abraham became fully persuaded that God was able to do what He had said He would do. Hebrews 11:11 Sarah judged God faithful to what He had promised.**

At the age of 90 she received strength to conceive and gave birth to the promised child, Isaac.

After only three months of calling himself and hearing himself called, father of many all day long, his 90-year-old wife conceived a child because they connected in FAITH. Abraham called things that be not as though they were until he BELIEVED it. Did God know what He was doing when He changed Abraham's name or what? Be like Abraham, say it until you BELIEVE it and you will have it too.

2 Corinthians 4:13 I BELIEVED therefore have I spoken.

Once you get to the point of BELIEVING, speak it and you will have it.

SOWING GOD'S WORD

Sowing God's Word is downloading God's Word into your heart.

In Mark Chapter 4 Jesus taught us about sowing God's Word and letting it grow. This is the same as confession.

Galatians 6:7 Do not be deceived, God is not mocked, whatever kind of seeds people sow, that is what they will reap.

Word seeds grow FAITH or FEAR according to the type of words you sow.

Your heart (The ground) will produce nothing until a seed is planted.

Seeds always produce after their own kind and words are no different. If you sow seeds of poverty you will grow FAITH for poverty. If you sow seeds of abundance you will grow FAITH for abundance. If you sow seeds of good health you will grow FAITH for good health.

Jesus said that the sower sows the Word and it grows while you sleep and while you are awake. The more of God's Word that you sow the greater the harvest.

Speaking God's Word over and over again is a process of sowing promises of God until they grow and produce. You do not need to understand how seeds grow but you do need to understand how to plant them.

To receive any promise of God you must develop FAITH to the point where you are fully persuaded, as Abraham was, according to Romans 4:21. Confessing will eventually cause that to happen.

The minute you begin to BELIVE what you are confessing, the connection is made and things will start to change. Eventually, you will possess what God has already provided for you.

The secret is to just keep sowing God's promise over and over again, in your heart, by speaking it out of your mouth, for as long as it takes you to connect and you will eventually receive what you want or need.

THE FAITH CYCLE

When you speak God's Word you hear God's Word, and if you speak it enough times it will go down and be planted in your heart (Spirit). The more you speak it, the fuller your spirit gets.

Matthew 12:34 Jesus said, out of the abundance (Overflow) of the heart the mouth speaks.

Your spirit can only hold a certain amount of God's Word before it, like any other container, begins to overflow. Your mouth is the **overflow valve or spigot** for your spirit. When your spirit overflows, God's Word starts coming out of your mouth. The first person to hear it is you and it goes right back down into your spirit. Since your spirit is already full, it will come up again and pour out of your mouth. The more you cycle God's Word, the stronger your FAITH gets and things begin to change according to the kind of seeds, of God's Words, you are planting into your spirit.

If you are cycling God's Words on healing, your body will begin to heal. If you are cycling God's Words on increase and abundance that is what will eventually happen in your life.

Seed once planted, usually do not grow overnight. It is a process.

Genesis 8:22 As long as the earth is here there will be seedtime and harvest.

The more of God's Word that you hear, the more it is planted into your heart, and the more harvest it produces in your life.

NEGATIVE WORDS

Proverbs 18:21 Your tongue has the power of life and death over you and you will live by the words that come out of your mouth.

Many people want success and abundance, but are speaking negative words about themselves. Because of that they are sowing failure and poverty into their lives. Other people want good health, but consistently plant word seeds of sickness and disease.

Whatever type of words you sow into your heart, they will eventually grow, produce a harvest and change your life. Be careful with your words.

Mark 4:24 Be careful what you listen to.

Jesus said this because He knows that the words that you hear will cause FAITH or FEAR to be sown into your heart.

The more of God's Word that you hear, the less FEAR you will have in your life.

BULLDOG FAITH

A Bulldog holding onto a bone, or anything else, has a very high **determination factor**. I had an English Bulldog, named John. When he grabbed ahold of something you might as well let go and go to bed. It was his.

1 Timothy 6:12, the Apostle Paul told the young Pastor, Timothy, to fight the good fight of FAITH, lay hold of (Grab onto) eternal life. That is also what you should do with all of God's promises.

What you speak you hear, and what you continually hear you will eventually BELIEVE.

You can only hear something, anything, **a certain number of times** until you start to BELIEVE it. I tell people who are trying to increase their FAITH, "**Your number** is out there, find it." Say it until you get it!!!

MY DETERMINATION FACTOR

In November of 2012, I received a revelation that THE BLESSING OF ABRAHAM was my inheritance. I knew that it belonged to me. I wanted it and I was determined to have it. However, I just did not know how to get it to come upon me.

I had FAITH for THE BLESSING. The problem was the fact that my FAITH for THE BLESSING was HEAD FAITH, not HEART FAITH, and I knew it. I started a program of sowing FAITH for THE BLESSING into my heart.

I started saying "THE BLESSING OF ABRAHAM is my inheritance, now Lord, You BLESS me." I intended to say this 100 times every day. I even had the people in our church saying it. I said this over and over again, all day long, every day. I estimate that I said it 300 to 500 times a day. I did this, day after day, week after week and month after month for 8 months. I spoke this for 240 days X 300 times per day = 72,000 times, at least. I was determined to have THE BLESSING come upon me.

In June of 2013 the Lord spoke to me in an audible voice and told me what to do to get THE BLESSING OF ABRAHAM to come upon me. Of course, I quickly did what God told me to do. In only five months, our debt of $295,000 went away, evaporated. We now live an abundant, debt free happy life with no stress. Thousands of other people have also received THE BLESSING because of what The Lord taught me.

It took me eight months to connect in FAITH with God for THE BLESSING. You do not have to spend eight months doing what I did, because I now know how to get THE BLESSING OF ABRAHAM to actually come upon a person, ANY PERSON!

Creflo Dollar was diagnosed with an aggressive form of prostate cancer. He went into a room with the intention of increasing his FAITH for healing. After two weeks he connected in FAITH, came out, went back to the doctor, and was told that there was no sign of cancer. That is **Bulldog determination!**

What is your determination factor when it comes to receiving from God? Are you like John, the **bulldog**? I am. So are many others. If you have BULLDOG FAITH, you will receive from God every time.

THE SHORT CUT

Find the promise of God that pertains to what you want or need and speak it over yourself until you connect in FAITH. Combine it with a demanding prayer, stay with it and it works every time.

Developing FAITH in Proverbs 3:9-10 kept us in Bible College after we had run out of money. We were BROKE!

We had Fifty-Eight Cents left in our bank account with rent coming up and tuition due in a few days. I needed to quickly increase my FAITH. At 6 AM on a Thursday morning I read

Proverbs 3:9-10, Honor the Lord with your substances and the first fruits of all your increase. So, your barns will be filled with plenty.

I said to the Lord, "I have honored You with the first fruits of all my increase and my barns are not full. Now You do what You said You will do!" I said that over and over and over again for several hours. Finally, I sat down. I knew I had it. I had connected in FAITH.

That afternoon our finances broke wide open. Money started coming from several different directions and we had plenty of money for school and all of our bills. We were even able to help other people with their tuition.

Another time, I woke up at 7 AM with a kidney stone. The pain was very intense. I started saying. "Lord, Your Word says I was healed by the Stripes of Jesus, (1 Peter 2:24), now You heal me." I said that over and over again, sometime very loud, until 2 PM when the Lord spoke to me and said, "I am going to heal you." A few hours later I was totally healed.

THE GIFT OF FAITH

This is a gift of the Holy Spirit, whereby a Believer is empowered by God with special FAITH to do something, or receive something. It is usually for a specific situation. This gift can cause you to receive a needed miracle.

Daniel had a supernatural gift of FAITH, for protection, when he was thrown into the den of lions. The gift of FAITH will give you a sense of calm in the face of danger.

The gift of FAITH can be used by God to encourage us. This happened to me one evening while I was increasing my FAITH to receive THE BLESSING. I was driving the car into the garage, while confessing that THE BLESSING OF ABRAHAM is my inheritance. All of a sudden, I felt something drop down into my spirit and I knew beyond any doubt, that soon I was going to get THE BLESSING. A couple of months later I received it. That was a gift of FAITH.

The gift of FAITH can be given by God so people can accomplish a task, start a new business, for success in your job, or anything else you are trying to do.

It seems to me that people who are trying to increase their FAITH for something are the ones most likely to receive the gift of FAITH from God.

THE FAITH CHALLENGE

If you confess any promise of God 100 times a day for 90 days, in all likelihood, it is going to begin manifesting in your life. Pick a promise of God, healing, abundance, favor or anything, confess it 100 times a day for 90 days and watch what happens. For even better results, combine it with a demanding prayer.

Examples of demanding prayers:

Lord, Your Word says I was healed by the Stripes of Jesus, so you heal me now.

Lord, Your Word says I was made rich by the poverty of Jesus, so you increase my finances now.

Lord, Your Word says that THE BLESSING OF ABRAHAM is my inheritance, so you BLESS me now.

Find the promise and speak the promise until you have the promise.

The strength of your FAITH is determined by the amount of time you spend hearing God's Word and the stronger your FAITH the more you get from God.

FAITH IN DIFFERENT AREAS

FAITH FACT: FAITH for salvation will not heal you or increase your finances.

FAITH FACT: FAITH for abundance will not heal your body.

FAITH FACT: FAITH to speak healing over other sick people will not heal you.

Understanding this principle of FAITH will allow you to increase your FAITH in the area where you have a need. Very few people know that FAITH is different in each area of their life. They think that a person either has FAITH or they don't. The truth of the matter is that they might have GREAT FAITH in one area of their life and little or no FAITH in other areas.

This explains why people can sometimes live in good health and be broke at the same time, or vice versa. Most Jewish people have GREAT FAITH for the BLESSING OF ABRAHAM and so live in absolute abundance, financially. At the same time, many of them do not seem to have FAITH for God's healing and so have health problems.

This also explains why many Christians, who have GREAT FAITH for salvation are sick and broke. We have always had GREAT FAITH for our health but were broke because we had only HEAD FAITH for our finances. When I realized what the problem was, everything began to change.

Many wonderful men and women of God, who had GREAT FAITH to heal the sick, died of sickness and disease themselves, or had members of their family die before their time. They did not realize that they needed to increase their FAITH for themselves and their own families.

In my own case, I had FAITH to speak THE BLESSING over other people and our children for years before I understood why I was struggling with my own finances. People in our church were receiving huge financial BLESSINGS and our children were very successful and living abundant lives, but we were broke. I discovered that our problem was **my lack of FAITH** for our own finances. I started increasing MY FAITH for **our finances** and THE BLESSING, and now we also live in abundance.

I can always tell what a person has FAITH for because of what is going on in each area of their life. If someone is living an abundant life I know it is because they have FAITH for abundance. If they are broke, it is because they have no FAITH for their finances. If they are sick all the time, it is because they have no FAITH for healing and so on. You can stop questioning why things are the way they are in your life, or the life of anyone else. It is **always** a FAITH issue.

You do not need to have GREAT FAITH in every area of your life to live a victorious life. Just knowing how to increase your FAITH in any given area, when the need arises, will keep you from ever being defeated. You can pick any area of your life, increase your FAITH and increase your standard of life in that area any time you want to.

If you get sick, work on increasing your FAITH for healing. If you need finances, work on increasing your FAITH for finances. Do not be deceived by how simple this is.

FAITH TO RECEIVE

FAITH FACT: God never picks out people to SAVE, HEAL or BLESS.

FAITH FACT: Everything you receive from God, you receive according to Faith.

FAITH FACT: Owning something and possessing something are two different things.

FAITH FACT: There are two ways to receive from God. Through your FAITH or the FAITH of someone else.

Using FAITH to receive from God is like using money to buy food at the Super Market. The more money you take with you the more food you can get. With God, the higher your level of FAITH, the more you get from Him.

God will never ever do anything for anyone under any circumstances, unless someone involved in the request, BELIEVES that **He is able** and EXPECTS that **He will do it**. No exceptions.

John 19:30 Jesus said, "It is finished" and He bowed His head and gave up His spirit.

He meant that there was nothing left for Him to do here on earth. Jesus has already done everything that He is ever going to do for us, in order for us to possess all of the promises of God. Now all we need to do, is to receive them by FAITH.

FAITH to receive from God is based on **EXPECTING** God to give you what He has promised and **BELIEVING** that He actually **is able** to do it.

Romans 10:9-10 BELIEVE in your heart and confess with your mouth and you shall have salvation.

That is also how we receive everything else we get from God. You must get to the point where you EXPECT it and speak it and then you will have it.

Matthew 8:13 Jesus said to the centurion, go your way and as you have EXPECTED, be it done for you.

THE PROSPEROUS SOUL

3 John 2 Beloved, above all things, it is my wish that you prosper and be in health even as your soul prospers.

You will prosper and be in health at the **same rate** that your soul, (Your mind and spirit) prospers. Therefore, it is very important to try to enrich, or strengthen your soul by feeding it God's Word. My 15 Minute videos will prosper your soul, when you watch them every day.

FAITH OVERCOMES

There is no problem, situation or circumstance too big, or too overwhelming for a person with FAITH. In 1 Samuel 17, David was standing in front of a giant who wanted to kill him. He was able to kill the giant because he BELIEVED that God was able to deliver him and he EXPECTED God to give him the victory over this non-covenant person. David said,

> **1Samuel 17:26 Who is this non-covenant person that he would have the audacity to defy the armies of the living God.**

TWO THINGS YOU MUST BELEIVE

In order to connect in FAITH and receive from God, you must believe these two things. You must BELIEVE that God **is able** and EXPECT that **He will** do what you ask of Him.

Here is the perfect example of how we must BELIEVE in order to connect in FAITH and receive from God.

> **Daniel 3:17 Shadrach, Meshach, and Abednego said, if you throw us into the fiery furnace, our God is able and He will deliver us from your hand, O King.**

The king then had them thrown into the furnace and God did indeed deliver them out, completely unharmed, just as they **had spoken**. Situations and circumstances do not get any worse than that.

A person who BELIEVES that God **is able** and EXPECTS that **God will**, with no doubt whatsoever, is going to receive every time, without fail and without delay, no matter what the situation is.

ACCORDING TO YOUR FAITH

Matthew 9:29 Jesus touched their eyes and said, according to your FAITH, be it unto you.

Many people believe that God passes out His Blessings, healings and promises randomly, but the absolute brutal truth is the fact that we **only** receive from God **according to our FAITH**.

2 Peter 1:2 Grace and peace will abound to you through the revelation knowledge (FAITH) of God and of Jesus our Lord.

This means, the more FAITH you have in God and Jesus, the more grace and peace you get from God.

If people receive little, it's because they have LITTLE FAITH, or revelation knowledge. If they doubt, they receive nothing according to James 1:6-7

Another way of saying this is, the amount of grace and peace and everything else, that you receive from God, is in direct proportion to the amount of revelation knowledge and FAITH you have in God and Jesus.

Therefore, it makes good sense to me that anyone who would like to increase what they are receiving from God, should be trying to increase their revelation knowledge and FAITH in God and Jesus. HUH?

EXPECT TO RECEIVE

Mark 11:24 Jesus said, therefore I say unto you, anything you desire when you pray, EXPECT to receive them and you will have them.

No matter what you are BELIEVING God for, you must EXPECT to get it **before** you get it, or it will never happen.

All of the BLESSINGS AND promises of God come through FAITH. You will receive **only the ones** that you EXPECT to receive.

A man was healed in Acts 14:7-10 because he heard Paul preach, (apparently about healing) developed his FAITH to be healed and stood up when Paul told him to.

In Genesis Chapter 27, FAITH in THE BLESSING, caused Jacob to become **Spiritually Empowered for Success**. It will do the same for you.

You must hear a Promise of God in order to BELIEVE it. You must BELIEVE and act on it, or speak a promise of God in order to receive it.

Everyone wants to think, and many people teach, that God BLESSES all people the same, but that is simply not the case. Some people believe God provides for and BLESSES people according to their needs. Again, not the case.

The truth of the matter is, without FAITH, God will allow you to go broke, to get sick and die of disease, and even die and go to hell. But with FAITH God will save your soul, heal your body, pay your bills, and bring you to a happy, stress free place where you are living in abundance.

FAITH REMOVES LIMITATIONS

Mark 9:23 Jesus said, if you are able to BELIEVE, anything is possible to any person who BELIEVES.

By this verse we know that there is nothing we cannot have, nowhere we cannot go, and nothing we cannot achieve, if only we have FAITH for it. You have no limitations on your life, if only you can BELIEVE God's Word and what He says about you.

In Genesis Chapter 26, FAITH in what God told him caused Isaac to become very rich, even to the point where his enemies were afraid of him. This happened during a famine while Isaac and his family were surrounded by the Philistines. This proves that FAITH in God's Word removes all limitations on a person's life, even in the most severe circumstances.

BE A GRABBER

Numbers 33:53 God said, I have given you the land to possess it.

Just because God has given us something does not mean we will ever possess it. According to 1 Timothy 6:12 We must take hold (Grab tightly) of eternal life and that also applies to everything else that God has already given us.

When God gave Abraham the land, 400 years earlier, they owned it. However, owning something and possessing it are two different things. Because of what Jesus has done for us, the covenant, eternal salvation, healing, forgiveness, THE BLESSING, abundance and all the promises of God already belong to us. I have to ask, how many of God's promises do you own? The answer, all of them. Now, how many do you actually possess?" You probably possess eternal salvation and that is wonderful, but how about the rest?

WILDERNESS LIVING

Jesus was in the wilderness for forty days where he was tempted by the devil. He countered every temptation by speaking the Word of God.

The children of Israel spent forty years living in the wilderness, where God provided manna and everything else they needed, on a day to day basis. Almost everyone over the age of twenty died there, because of UNBELIEF, never having entered the promised land. They were afraid of the giants and the high walls in the promised land. They doubted that they would be able to possess the land.

High walls and giants did not keep the children of Israel out of the promised land, but UNBELIEF did. Forty years later, the next generation, full of FAITH, crossed the flooded raging river on dry ground, shouted down the walls, killed the giants and took possession of the land.

People have developed what we call a **Wilderness, or Poverty Mentality** where they expect to struggle every day just to make ends meet. They are always fearful of running out of money, getting sick, or not having enough of what they need to get by. This is not how God intended for His people to live.

Many Christians are still living in the wilderness today with their wilderness mentalities. They live paycheck to paycheck, day to day, week to week and month to month, never having received THE BLESSING that Jesus made them eligible for. He has already redeemed all of us from the curse of the law. Unfortunately, most of them die in the wilderness, and go to Heaven, without ever reaching the fullness of God's BLESSING here on earth.

RENEW YOUR MIND

Romans 12:2 Do not be conformed to this world but be transformed by the renewing of your minds so you will know what is good and acceptable and the perfect will of God.

Renewing your mind is how you change your wilderness mentality into a BLESSING mentality. When that happens, your life will begin to change for the better.

A wonderful lady in our church, Evelisse Feijoo said, "See yourself the way God sees you and love yourself the way God loves you." That is where we all need to be. Renewing your mind, through God's Word will get you to that place.

My ministry is all about how to possess the promises of God, especially salvation, healing and THE BLESSING. That is why they call me 'The how-to preacher." It does not do you any good to just know about God's promises unless you also learn how to possess them.

2 Corinthians 13:5 Examine yourselves to see if you be in the FAITH.

We should also examine our FAITH concerning every area of our lives.

The stronger your FAITH, the quicker the promises of God will manifest in your life.

With God, receiving always comes after EXPECTING, never before.

Every promise of God is true. All you need to do to receive it for yourself is develop your FAITH.

THE CONNECTION

In order for anyone to receive anything from God, someone must connect in FAITH, by BELIEVING that God is able and EXPECTING that God will do it. You must be willing to do whatever it takes to make that connection.

The spilt second you connect in FAITH, things will begin to happen, sometimes slowly at first. You will begin to receive whatever it is that you want or need from God. Your body will begin to heal, THE BLESSING will come upon you, prayers will be answered, debt will begin to evaporate and fear, anxiety and stress will leave your life.

WHY PEOPLE FAIL TO RECEIVE

FAILURE FACT: Failure to receive is never God's fault.

FAILURE FACT: Failure to receive is never because God says no.

FAILURE FACT: Failure to receive is **always a lack of FAITH**.

When most people fail to receive from God, they wrongfully assume that it is not God's will for them to have it.

Hebrews 3:19 The children of Israel could not enter the Promised land because they did not BELIEVE that God **was able** to get them through safely.

The disciples ask Jesus in **Matthew 17:19-20, why could we not cast out the evil spirit. Jesus said, "Because of your unbelief."** The reason for failure is always unbelief.

There are three main reasons for UNBELIEF.

1. Ignorance, caused by not hearing God's Word. God has great mercy on these people and will always make a way for them to learn what they need to know. God has done this for me so many times that I cannot even count them. He has even spoken to me and told me where to find what I needed to know.

2. Refusal to BELIEVE, like Thomas in John chapter 20 and the Children of Israel in Numbers chapter 13. God has very little mercy on people who have heard and refuse to BELIEVE His Word.

3. SPOKEN DOUBT is a huge reason people develop unbelief and do not receive. I tell people this, "If doubt comes into your mind, keep your mouth shut and it will not interfere with your FAITH.

Proverbs 3:5 Trust in the Lord with all of your heart and do not depend on your own understanding.

Don't try to figure everything out about God's Word and how things are going to happen. Just BELIEVE that you will receive.

It seems that the majority of people who receive after being prayed for, do nothing but say thank you, then go about their business.

People who want to know when and how and keep fussing, whining and asking questions never seem to get anything from God. Also, people who keep praying after I pray for them or hunt for someone else to pray for them, never seem to receive. I ask people this question, "If Jesus Himself prayed over you, would you go home and pray about the same issue some more or try to find someone else to pray for you?" I don't think so.

EXAMINE YOUR FAITH

Don't overload your FAITH trying to BELIEVE for something you do not have enough FAITH for. Many people make this mistake. If there is something you want or need, ask yourself, do I have the FAITH for this? If you do not, then increase your FAITH until you are able to get it, or find someone to help you get it. How simple is that. HUH?

2 Corinthians 13:5 Examine yourself to determine if you be in FAITH.

We should always examine our FAITH before we approach God for anything we try to do, or for anything we want or need. I will do this before I pray about anything. When people call me to pray for them, I will examine my FAITH. If I do not have FAITH to help them receive what they want or need, I will tell them.

I always check to see if I have enough FAITH for what I want to do. I have gotten myself into big trouble because I did not have enough FAITH for what I was trying to do.

Many people are standing on FAITH that they do not have and wondering why they are not receiving from God.

If you have not yet received what you want or need from God, understand that the reason is always because your FAITH is not where it needs to be.

DO NOT BE OFFENDED

In Mark Chapter 6 Jesus went to His home area and was teaching, but could not perform miracles because the people were offended by Him. This was because He was a carpenter, whom they had known before His ministry started and they were full of UNBELIEF.

I have had cases where I could not help people because they were offended by the things God was doing through me. One was a pastor who refused to meet with me when he had cancer, even after Mary and I were invited to his house. He was offended by my healing ministry. He could have been healed, but he died.

Another is a healing evangelist who called me when he was sick. After I spoke healing over him, he was offended because I said, "Now that is the end of it, just relax and let your body heal." He posted and said, "I should just pray for people and leave the rest up to God." When I minister to a sick person I absolutely mean for that to be the end of their illness, and I don't hesitate to say so. That was months ago and he is still very ill. I prayed for him to have wisdom.

UNFORGIVENESS

Mark 11:25 When you stand to pray, forgive if you have anything against anyone.

Unforgiveness can be a huge obstacle to receiving from God. I don't think it is any coincidence that Jesus told us to forgive others, right after He taught us how to use our FAITH. If you are having trouble with this, ask God to help you forgive others. Another good way to do it is that every time you think about a person who has done bad things to you, speak BLESSINGS over them. Forgiveness will soon come and you will be free.

Hebrews 12:15 Be careful that no one falls short of the grace of God, that no root of bitterness springing up cause trouble and by it, many be defiled.

A few years ago, a 78-year-old lady, who had harbored unforgiveness all of her life, was able to forgive after I taught about removing the root of bitterness. Two years after that, she was dying of heart failure in the ICU and her husband called me to come. I commanded her heart to be healed on a Thursday morning. She got up from her hospital bed and went home that evening, completely healed. Sunday morning, she was in church telling everyone what had happened.

EXCUSES FOR NOT RECEIVING

1. "God's timing is perfect." I have known people who said this for years while they suffered sickness, poverty and lack. I have noticed over the years that God's timing always coincides with your FAITH. The stronger your FAITH, the quicker you get results.

2. "God must know that I am not ready for it." If you can BELIEVE for something, God will give it to you whether you are ready for it or not.

3. "God must not want me to have it." He gave Israel a king and He certainly did not want them to have one.

4. And the most popular excuse for not receiving, "We are just going to leave it in God's Hands." Sick people who say this never seem to get healed.

Increase your FAITH and you will not need an excuse for not receiving.

THE EASY WAY TO RECEIVE

If your FAITH is not where it needs to be, in order to receive from God, find someone who does have enough FAITH to agree in prayer with you. My prayer partners do this every day and receive what they want or need.

FAITH FOR ABUNDANCE

FAITH FACT: God does not pick out people to BLESS.

FAITH FACT: Neither poverty nor prosperity is about money.

John 10:10 Jesus said, I have come that you may have a life which is super abundant.

The word abundant means more than enough. I said for years that I would never be satisfied until I was living in the abundance that Jesus came to provide for us.

Our God is not a God of enough, He is a too much God.

Psalm 23:5 David said, my cup runs over.

Question, why does God run the cup over? Answer, because that is the kind of God He is.

In Luke Chapter 5, Jesus filled the nets of Simon so full that the nets broke and the boats began to sink. Question, why would

God give Simon more fish than he could handle? Answer, because that is the kind of God He is.

Our God is a cup running over, net breaking, boat sinking, BLESSING God.

FAITH FOR THE BLESSING

Galatians 3:13-14 Christ has redeemed us from the curse of the law so that THE BLESSING of Abraham can come upon the Gentiles. All born again people are redeemed but THE BLESSING, just like all other promises of God, must be received by FAITH.

Many people believe that THE BLESSING is automatic, but if that is true, why are so many Christians broke?

Proverbs 10:22 THE BLESSING OF THE LORD it makes a person rich and God adds no toil (Hard work) to it.

No one, who has THE BLESSING of God upon them stays broke.

The word rich being defined, according to **2 Corinthians 9:8**, as having all sufficiency to meet your needs with plenty left over. That means more than enough to live on, with extra money to help good causes.

85% of the Jewish people live in absolute abundance because they BELIEVE that they are the chosen people of God, sons and daughters of Abraham and they have FAITH for THE BLESSING OF ABRAHAM. All born again people are also sons and daughters of Abraham and are also eligible to receive THE BLESSING.

NOT ABOUT MONEY

Poverty and failure are part of the curse of the law.

Deuteronomy 28:29 You shall try to feel your way around during the daylight, as the blind gropes in darkness, and you shall not prosper in your ways and you shall be only oppressed and ruined forever (Generational) and no one will be able to help you.

When we break the spirit of poverty and remove all generational curses of poverty and failure, people began to see increase in only a short while.

The abundant life is a result of THE BLESSING OF ABRAHAM and poverty is usually caused by a generational curse of poverty, or a spirit of poverty.

When people who call me, or come to my church, are having financial problems, I do not tell them to change their spending habits. I rebuke the generational curse of poverty and the curse of poverty that is affecting their life. If they then watch their words, their finances will begin to increase in a short while and sometimes very quickly.

If you are having financial problems, start a program of increasing your FAITH for THE BLESSING.

Mary and I struggled with our finances for years. We had to use all the FAITH we had just to get enough money to pay our bills at the end of every month. The worse day of the month for me, the day I would dread, was the day we had to sit down and pay the bills. One day I was sitting in the office and I got a huge revelation. I called for Mary to come back there and I said to her, "I now know why we are having so much trouble with our finances." She said, "Why is that?" I replied, "Because I do not have enough FAITH." She said, "Well, get the FAITH." I said, "I will."

I began a program of reading God's Word about prosperity and abundance out loud and listening to good preaching on that subject, usually 4 or 5 hours per day. Day after day, week after week, month after month and yes, year after year. Mary kept asking me, "When is this going to work?" I would tell her, "I don't know, but I do know that God's Word works and I know I am on the right track.

Finally, things began to change. God gave me revelations of what I needed to do. First, I needed to get my words under control. Then He also showed me other things, such as breaking the spirit of poverty and the generational curse of poverty, that had been running in my family for years. That I also needed to break the curse of the law and lastly, how to receive THE BLESSING of Abraham upon my life.

Mary and I have never lived like we are living right now. To borrow a phrase from Dr. Leroy Thompson, "I will never be broke another day in my life."

If you are determined enough, there is nothing you cannot receive from God including abundance. All you have to do is increase your faith by hearing God's Word until you get it.

BE GENEROUS

Proverbs 11:25 A person who is generous will prosper.

There are two kinds of people, takers and givers. Takers have little FAITH. They depend on other people. Givers live a life of FAITH and give at every opportunity because money and possessions are not important to them. They BELIEVE, "God never runs out, so there is more where that came from."

When a taker turns into a giver, their life will begin to change and they will soon be living in abundance.

FAITH FOR HEALING

FAITH FACT: There is so much sickness among Christians because of a lack of FAITH for healing.

FAITH FACT: It is always God's will to heal everyone, without exception.

FAITH FACT: God does not pick out people to heal.

FAITH FACT: God does not heal anyone because they need to be healed.

FAITH FACT: It is not a lack of FAITH to go to the doctor.

In order to be healed, you must refuse to accept sickness in your body.

You must know God's will before you can develop FAITH for healing.

Many years ago, Kenneth Hagin established a healing school on the campus of Rhema Bible College. He began teaching the will of God concerning healing and good health. Many people were wonderfully healed just sitting in their seats, without even being prayed for. We were there when some of that took place. Others were healed when they were prayed for. The Rhema healing school is still operating there today and getting the same results. If you are sick and can't seem to receive your healing, go there!

When people get a revelation of God's will concerning healing, or anything else for that matter, they become much more receptive to receiving from God.

James 5:15 and the prayer of FAITH shall heal the sick and the Lord shall raise them up.

This is the only prayer that will heal sick people.

The brutal truth is that God will never, ever, under any circumstances, heal anyone unless His requirement of FAITH is met. Everyone who has ever died of sickness or disease has done so because they, or the people around them, did not have FAITH for their healing. This includes many prominent, wonderful and powerful men and women of God, who have had great ministries and who were a BLESSING to thousands of people.

When anyone, no matter who they are, dies of sickness or disease it is **always because they did not have FAITH for their healing**. There is never any other reason and it is never God's fault. God does not pick out people to make sick or die.

The rule is: Never base your faith on what has happened to another person, any person, no matter who they are. Just because someone, who was considered a great person of FAITH, did not get healed, does not in the least mean that God will not heal you. If you meet His requirement of FAITH, you most certainly will be healed, without fail and without delay.

However, when someone does get a healing miracle it is always because either they, or someone ministering to them, has met God's requirement of FAITH.

BAD ADVICE

James 3:1 There should not be many teachers because they will be held accountable.

When you jump in and try to minister healing to a sick person, you very well may be held responsible for the outcome.

A very well know man in our area was sick for five years and did not go to see a doctor. His "Spiritual" friends told him that indicates a "Lack of FAITH" even though he had extreme pain in his abdomen.

By the time he asked me to help him, he was full of cancer, totally confused and angry. I tried to increase his FAITH by getting him to listen to God's Word on healing but his friends jumped in again and convinced him that was the wrong approach. They told him he already had enough FAITH to be healed. He decided that they were right I was wrong and he dismissed me as his Pastor. Two days later he died a horrible death in a room full of crying people.

Less than a month later, the daughter of his "Spiritual friends" fell out of a tree and broke her arm. Of course, they took her to the hospital right away and had a cast put on her arm. **Where was their FAITH?** It was a much different story when their own child was suffering. Turns out that his "Spiritual friends" did not even BELIEVE themselves what they were telling this poor man, who was so sick, in pain and put his FAITH in what they told him.

It is not a lack of FAITH to go to a doctor! I tell people this," Have the doctor treat the symptoms, which will make you feel better, but always look to God for your healing." Doctors are not healers, God is, but many of them are very good at treating symptoms. Let the doctor treat the symptoms while you are increasing your faith for healing.

Mix FAITH with your medicine. Every time you take a pill say," I am getting better every day.

Please keep in mind that most of the time, healing by the power of God is progressive. Once the spirit of infirmity (Sickness) is told to leave and healing has been spoken, or hands laid upon you, the healing power of God has entered your body and will bring about your healing. Complete healing may happen quickly or over a period of time and there is nothing more you need to do, or should try to do, to make it happen.

How healing happens is up to God, although I have noticed that the stronger the FAITH the quicker the healing. I have spoken over 3 people who were blind. One was healed in 30 days, another in 3 days and the third in two minutes. Once I minister to a sick person I do not even pretend to know how it is going to happen, but I do know it will.

Do not deny sickness, deny it's right to be in your body, because your body is the Temple of the Holy Ghost.

FAITH TO HEAL SICK PEOPLE

Acts 10:38 How God anointed Jesus of Nazareth with the Holy Ghost and with power who went around doing

**good and healing all who were oppressed with sickness
by the devil, because God was with Him.**

According to Luke 13:11-13 Jesus healed people by casting out
the spirit of infirmity and then laying his Hands on them. We also
know that in some cases Jesus just spoke over them. We are to do
the same thing but It takes Faith in THE NAME OF JESUS to do it.

GENERATIONAL CURSES OF SICKNESS

Doctors use the word "Hereditary" to describe diseases that
are passed down in families. They are actually generational curses.
Heart disease, of course is the big one. Also, cancer, diabetes, high
blood pressure, dementia, mental illness, osteoporosis and many
more. All of these can be found in Deuteronomy, chapter 28, as part
of the curse of the law.

Once these generational curses are broken through FAITH
IN THE NAME OF JESUS, people will begin to heal. Once again,
do not be deceived by how simple this is.

I never ask sick people if I can pray for them. Actually, I never
pray for sick people because Jesus never did. I command the spirit
of infirmity to leave and then I lay my hands on them and say, "Be
healed in the Name of Jesus." If we are talking on the phone I tell the
spirit of infirmity to leave them and then I just speak, "Be healed," to
their body. Works every time.

Several years ago, I walked into an insurance office to meet
with someone. The lady at the desk ask me if I had any aspirin with
me. I said, "No, why do you ask." She said she had a migraine head-
ache and was sick to her stomach. I said, "I have the perfect cure for
that if you want to get rid of it." She said, "Oh yes." I reached across

the desk, put my hand on her forehead and said, "In the Name of Jesus, come out of her. Now shake your head and say thank you Jesus." She did and her eyes popped wide open and she said, "It's gone." I said, "Of course it is."

THE PRAYER OF FAITH

FAITH FACT: God does not pick out prayers to answer.

FAITH FACT: The prayer of FAITH will save your soul, heal your body and pay your bills.

> **James 5:15-16 is anyone sick among you? let him call for the elders of the church; and let them pray over him, anointing him with oil in the name of the Lord: 15 And the prayer of faith shall save the sick, and the Lord shall raise him up; and if he has committed sins, they shall be forgiven him.**

The prayer of FAITH will also pay your bills.

The prayer of FAITH is actually the **Only Prayer** that God will ever answer. God will **NEVER, EVER** answer any prayer, no matter who is praying, how many people are praying, or what you are praying for, unless it is a prayer of FAITH.

A prayer of FAITH is a prayer, where the person praying, absolutely EXPECTS God to answer, without a shred of doubt.

The answer to your prayer never depends on God and there is never any possible failure on His part.

Prayers are never answered unless someone involved has FAITH.

Before you pray, think about what you are asking of God. Then upload your prayer and attach FAITH to it.

> **Mark 11:24 Jesus said, Therefore I say to you, whatever (Anything) you desire when you pray, EXPECT that you will receive it and you will have it.**

The only time prayers are ever answered by God is when people absolutely EXPECT them to be answered, with no doubt. All other prayers go unanswered.

People with GREAT FAITH will pray demanding prayers until they receive what they want or need. Example: Lord, Your Word says that I was healed by the stripes of Jesus so now you heal me, in THE NAME OF JESUS.

THE PRAYER OF HOPE

There is always a reason when prayers are not answered. An unanswered prayer is never God's fault. The reason for unanswered prayer is always because of a lack of FAITH. That is because people pray, but do not really expect God to answer their prayers, they just hope He might. God never answers a Prayer of Hope. If you are praying and hoping, you are wasting your time and God's.

FAITH to pray begins with understanding that God **wants** to answer your prayer. He is not moved by prayer groups, prayer chains, or even millions of people who may be praying for the same thing.

If you are born again you have a Blood bought, God given right to have your prayers answered. You also have a legal right to pray, if you use the Name of Jesus when you pray.

Before you ask God for anything, check your level of FAITH to determine if you have the FAITH for what you are asking. If you don't have enough FAITH, find someone who does and who will pray the prayer of agreement with you. My wonderful prayer ministry is based on the prayer of agreement and when I combine my FAITH with that of my prayer partners, we get amazing results.

Adding THE NAME OF JESUS to the end of your prayer does not guarantee success. However, when you add FAITH in that Name, you will have success every time.

FAITH IN
YOUR WORDS

FAITH FACT: If you say something, anything, about yourself and BELIEVE it, you will get it, good or bad.

FAITH FACT: If it is something good, ask God for it in THE NAME OF JESUS. If it is bad, tell it to leave in THE NAME OF JESUS.

> **Mark 11:22 Jesus answered and said to them, have FAITH like God has FAITH. The basic principle in this is, Romans 4:17 God who calls things which are not as if they were. BELIEVING with your heart and speaking with your mouth, as stated in Romans 10:9-10. Speak words of FAITH, like God does. When God speaks, He EXPECTS what He says to happen. We are supposed to operate the same way.**

In verse 23 Jesus said, **"For truly I say unto you, that anyone who speaks to this mountain (Problem, hindrance or obstacle)**

and tells it to go away and EXPECTS WITH NO DOUBT in his heart, that what he said will happen, he will have whatever he said.

The simple explanation of this verse is this, you can have whatever you say, if you say something and EXPECT it to happen, without any doubt.

We are not supposed to talk to God, or pray about problems and obstacles in our life. We are told to speak to them.

VOICE ACTIVATED

Paul told us in **Ephesians 5:1 be imitators of God as His beloved children.** Question, how do we imitate God? Answer, by operating like He operates, which according to **Romans 4:17 is calling those things that be not as if they were.**

In **Genesis 1:3 God looked into the darkness and said, "Light be."** However, there is something else that you need to get a revelation of in this passage of scripture. Look in verse 2, **The HOLY SPIRIT of God hovered over the face of the waters.** The HOLY SPIRIT was waiting for Almighty God to issue a command. When God said, "Light be" the HOLY SPIRIT moved and made it happen. I don't know if there was a "Big bang" or what, but I do know that what happened after God spoke was absolutely glorious and beyond anything we can ever imagine.

Healing is voice activated. Actually, everything we get from God is voice activated. THE BLESSING is also voice activated according to Numbers 6:22-27, Genesis 14:19 and Genesis 27:28-29

The HOLY SPIRIT is still hovering and waiting for someone who has FAITH IN THE NAME OF JESUS to speak a command. When that happens, He will move. That is how people get healed,

BLESSED, and prayers get answered through the power of His might, by someone speaking with FAITH IN THE NAME OF JESUS.

You issue a command in THE NAME OF JESUS with FAITH in that Name, and the HOLY SPIRIT will make it happen every time.

Jesus used his voice to activate the will of God while he was here on this earth. He looked at the storm and said, with GREAT FAITH, "Cease! be still." Jesus looked at sick people and said. "Be healed." He knew that He could make things happen with His words. We are supposed to operate the same way.

THE POWER OF HIS MIGHT

Ephesians 6:10 Finally, my brethren, be strong in the power of God's might.

This verse tells us that we can operate our lives and ministries in God's power, not just our own. A person operating in God's power can do what Jesus did, just like He said we could.

John 14:12 He that BELIEVES in me shall do the same works that I do and even more than I do because I go to my Father.

SPEAK THE WORD ONLY

Matthew 8:8 The centurion said to Jesus, "Lord, I am not worthy to have you come into my house but speak the Word only and my servant shall be healed."

Jesus said the centurion had GREAT FAITH.

You must develop FAITH in your own words. You must get to the point that when you make a command in THE NAME OF JESUS, you actually EXPECT, with no doubt, that what you say will happen. If you do, it will.

A person who operates in GREAT FAITH is a person who can say something and actually cause it to happen. Only people who have FAITH in their own words can do this. When I say something, IN THE NAME OF JESUS, I absolutely mean for it to happen.

> **Romans 10:6 The Word of FAITH, which we preach, is close to you, in your mouth and then in your heart.**

FAITH must be spoken by your mouth and then it goes into your heart in order for it to work. The FAITH in your heart is then activated by the words spoken by your mouth.

The process is Speak, and BELIEVE, then Speak and Receive, in that order.

FAITH FILLED WORDS

> **Hebrews 11:5 By FAITH we BELIEVE that God framed the world by His Words.**

God formed the world by speaking **FAITH FILLED WORDS.**

I guarantee you that God has absolute FAITH, that everything He says will happen and there is certainly no doubt in His Heart. When God said in Genesis 1:3 "Light be" what did He think was going to happen? Was God just trying out something, or did He actually mean for there to be light?

We are supposed to operate the same way as God, with FAITH FILLED WORDS. Jesus did and I am 100% sure that there was no doubt in His heart. When Jesus rebuked the wind in **Mark 5:39 and said, "Cease! be still"** what did He think was going to happen? Was Jesus just trying out something, or did He actually mean for the storm to stop? Every Word Jesus spoke was FAITH FILLED!

We are supposed to operate the same way that Jesus did because He told us to. John (14:12)

When I tell sickness to leave a person's body, in the Name of Jesus, I am not trying something. I mean for that sickness to leave right now and for that body to begin healing.

If we develop FAITH in the words that we speak, we can use them to frame our world. My world being my life, my family, my business, my church, my pets, my house, my possessions and my bank account. You can use FAITH FILLED WORDS to control these things. What do you think might happen if you spoke to your bank account and said, "Grow?" If you had developed FAITH in those words, your bank account would indeed grow.

BINDING AND LOOSING

These are the keys of the Kingdom of Heaven.

Matthew 18:19 Anything you bind (Prohibit) on earth is bound (Prohibited) from Heaven and anything you loose (Allow) on earth is loosed (allowed) from Heaven.

Every time we speak words in FAITH, either positive or negative, about ourselves, we are prohibiting something from being in our life, or allowing something in. We are to bind what is bad and loose what is good. For example, we should bind sickness from our lives and loose wealth and riches into our house as per Psalm 112:3

LIVE AN UNHINDERED LIFE

FAITH to keep the devil bound will result in you living an unhindered life with no obstacles to block your success. You can live an unhindered life.

Keep the devil bound from your life and you will be amazed by how much easier everything is for you. I do this every day in my own life, in the lives of the people in my church and my Prayer Partners.

Whatever we bind or loose in FAITH, here on earth, is bound or loosed from Heaven. Do not loose bad things into your life.

Positive words, spoken in FAITH, will cause God to move in your behalf. Negative words, spoken in FEAR, will cause the devil to move against you. Read Job chapter 1. Be careful what you say about yourself.

FAITH IN THE NAME OF JESUS

FAITH FACT: No one can live a victorious life without FAITH in THE NAME OF JESUS.

FAITH FACT: There is nothing you cannot have and nothing you cannot do if you have FAITH in THE NAME OF JESUS.

> **Philippians 2:10 At the NAME OF JESUS, the knee of every being in Heaven, on earth and under the earth shall bow.**

That was true when Jesus was on this earth. It is still true today and always will be true.

THE TRANSITION

The book of Acts is the transition from the ministry of Jesus and FAITH in JESUS, to the ministry of the BELIEVERS and FAITH in THE <u>NAME</u> OF JESUS.

Jesus gave us **power of attorney** to use His Name until He comes back. He certainly is coming back, we just don't know when, no one does. Now all of the promises and BLESSINGS of God come to us, through His Wonderful Name.

> **Mark 16:17 These signs (Miracles) shall follow (Only) those people who have FAITH in My Name. They shall cast out devils; they shall speak with new tongues. They will place their hands upon sick people and they will recover.**

This is the correct punctuation of this verse, according to the original Aramaic translation of the scriptures. When you read this verse the way it was originally punctuated, it makes a huge difference. We know that Jesus wants us to have FAITH in His Name and when we do, miracles will follow us.

There are a lot of things that are important to put your FAITH in but without a doubt the most important, is THE NAME OF JESUS.

Suggestion: instead of trying to BELIEVE for all kinds of different things, concentrate your FAITH in THE NAME OF JESUS, and all of these things will be much easier to get. Do not be deceived by how simple this is.

Jesus is now in Heaven and is not coming back until His appointed time. Romans 10:6-7 tells us not to even try to get Him to come down from Heaven or to come up from the dead. Jesus is not going to touch us with His Hand. He is not going to speak the Word over us. He is not going to cast the spirit of infirmity out of us when we are sick. We cannot touch the hem of His garment. But, we do have His Name to use.

We are commanded to have FAITH in The Name of Jesus (1 John 3:23)

When Jesus was here on earth, FAITH in Jesus and His ability would connect people to the power of God. Now that Jesus is in Heaven, it is FAITH in His Name that connects us to the power of God.

HEALING THE SICK

Every time Jesus sent people out to preach the Kingdom, He told them to also heal the sick.

Peter explains how the man at the Gate Beautiful received a healing miracle in **Acts 3:16** when he said, **"And His Name, through FAITH in the Name of Jesus has healed this man whom you see and know."**

Peter did not say that Jesus healed the lame man. He said it was FAITH IN THE NAME OF JESUS, that healed him.

> **Acts 4:30 That signs and wonders (Miracles) may be done in the NAME OF JESUS.**

Now, instead of having FAITH in Jesus for healing or anything else, we **MUST redirect our FAITH**, to His Name.

The secret to FAITH that causes MIRACLES, is FAITH in the NAME OF JESUS. That is why He gave us power of attorney to use His Wonderful and Powerful Name.

According to Mark 16:17 that is how all healing miracles (Signs) happen, through **FAITH IN THE NAME OF JESUS.**

Let me say it this way. In every healing miracle there must be someone involved who has **FAITH IN THE NAME OF JESUS.**

THE ONLY KEY TO MIRACLES

The truth of the matter is that miracles will **ONLY** follow people who have GREAT FAITH in the Name of Jesus. **Mark 16:17 These Signs (Miracles) shall follow (ONLY) them who have FAITH in My Name.**

Two of the miracles, Jesus talked about are casting out devils (Demons) and laying hands on the sick and having them recover.

People talk about seeking God's anointing for miracles but everyone I have ever seen or known of, who was anointed for miracles and healing, also had GREAT FAITH in the Name of Jesus. Develop your FAITH in THE NAME OF JESUS and the anointing will be there every time. Most people think that the healing evangelists, during the healing revival, had a special anointing for healing. I'm not sure about that, but I do know that they all had GREAT FAITH in THE NAME OF JESUS.

The Name of Jesus, when used with **GREAT FAITH,** carries the same power that Jesus Himself did when He was here on this earth 2,000 years ago. There is absolutely no difference in power between Jesus speaking over a sick person then, or a person using the Name of Jesus with GREAT FAITH, speaking over a sick person, now!

The key to making MIRACLES happen when you speak is FAITH IN THE NAME OF JESUS and that is the only way.

Many Christians BELIEVE that it takes a special anointing from God to heal the sick, when in fact, anyone with FAITH IN THE NAME OF JESUS can heal sick people. Here is another way of looking at Mark 16:17 **These signs (Miracles) shall follow them (All of them) who have FAITH IN My Name.**

A person with GREAT FAITH in the name of Jesus is a person who absolutely BELIEVES without any doubt, that when they use that Name, whatever they speak over, or pray for, is going to happen without fail and without delay. There are people who have that kind of GREAT FAITH in the Name of Jesus, but unfortunately, not many. There should be!

Every answered prayer, every miracle healing, every BLESSING spoken, and every promise of God received, are all a result of someone having GREAT FAITH in the Name of Jesus.

The truth of the matter is that every Christian has a legal right to use the Name of Jesus and almost all of them do, especially when they pray. However, very few people operate at a level of GREAT FAITH in that Name. Those that do are the people who get results on a consistent basis.

In order to get results, either a person must have FAITH in THE NAME OF JESUS themselves, or agree with someone who does.

THE WEAPON

1 John 3:8 For this purpose Jesus appeared on earth to destroy the works of the devil.

My purpose is to use His name, the weapon He gave us to use, to continue His work of destroying the works of the devil. This is what He commissioned us to do.

The NAME OF JESUS is a weapon that is more powerful than anything the devil can ever use against you.

Every born-again Christian has a Blood bought, God given right to use THE NAME OF JESUS, but only those who actually have FAITH IN THAT NAME will get results! Those are the people who EXPECT that when they use THAT NAME, what they say or pray for will happen. I am in that **small group** of people.

PERSONAL PROTECTION

Jesus did not want us to be defenseless after He left the earth and went to Heaven. He wanted us to be able to protect ourselves from sickness, disease, poverty and all matters of evil, so He left us with a weapon, **the weapon**, His Name.

Proverbs 18:10 The Name of the Lord is a strong tower, (Place of protection) the righteous run to it and are safe.

The NAME OF JESUS is the weapon that Jesus left with us for personal protection. Those who have GREAT FAITH in that Name, and know how to use it are **safe.**

If you do not have GREAT FAITH in the NAME OF JESUS, stay connected with someone who does, like your Pastor, or a Prayer Partner and they can provide protection for you.

WHEN TO USE THE NAME OF JESUS

- To heal yourself or others.
- To stop storms in your life.
- For financial increase and abundance.
- To break the power of the devil.
- Supernatural protection.
- To break generational curses

- To break the curse of the law

- To break the curse of poverty

- When you pray.

- To remove obstacles in your life.

- To speak THE BLESSING.

FAITH
IS TRANSFERABLE

FAITH Fact: If your FAITH is not where it needs to be, you can use the FAITH of someone else, who will combine their FAITH with yours, in the Prayer of Agreement.

FAITH FACT: My FAITH will work every time for people who have FAITH in my ability to get what they need for them.

If I want or need something from God, I do not care whose FAITH I have to use to get it.

I heard someone say "If I can't get it with my own FAITH I don't want it." That is pride and that person may not get anything from the Lord.

One afternoon, a few years ago I was home alone and reading in the book of Acts, Chapter 3.

Acts 3:1-8 Now Peter and John went up together to the temple at the hour of prayer, the ninth *hour*.[2] And a

certain man lame from his mother's womb was carried, whom they laid daily at the gate of the temple which is called Beautiful, to ask alms from those who entered the temple;[3] who, seeing Peter and John about to go into the temple, asked for alms.[4] And fixing his eyes on him, with John, Peter said, "Look at us."[5] So he gave them his attention, expecting to receive something from them.[6] Then Peter said, "Silver and gold I do not have, but what I do have I give you: In the name of Jesus Christ of Nazareth, rise up and walk."[7] And he took him by the right hand and lifted *him* up, and immediately his feet and ankle bones received strength.[8] So he, leaping up, stood and walked and entered the temple with them, walking, leaping, and praising God.

Then I read verse 16 **And His Name, through FAITH in His name (The Name of Jesus), has made this man strong, whom you see and know.**

The Lord spoke to me, inside my belly, in an audible voice and said, "Who had FAITH in the Name of Jesus?" I literally could not catch my breath. I let out a loud WHOA. The Lord God had asked me a question.

I did not answer right away as I wanted to get this right, so I reread the passage ten more times. About thirty minutes later I said, "Lord, it was not the man who was healed, it was **only** Peter who had FAITH in the Name of Jesus." The Lord did not speak to me again, but I knew I was right.

When Mary and Jean got home, they could see right away that I was very excited about something. I told them what had happened and we started to make a list of all the people we could think of who had been healed, or who had prayers answered that we knew had very little or no FAITH. Finally, we gave up. There were scores that we remembered and many, many more, so many that we could not even remember their names.

A few days later, the Lord showed me Matthew **18:19, where Jesus said, again I say to you that if two of you should agree concerning any desire that they might ask, it shall be done for them by My Father who is in Heaven.**

I realized that all of these people getting healed and having their prayers answered was based on the prayer of agreement. Many of them did not have any FAITH, but someone had to and in this case that was me.

A FAITH BOOST

Remember, to receive anything from God, someone must connect in FAITH, by BELIEVING that God **is able** and EXPECTING that He **will do it**.

Most people do not get their prayers answered and the reason is always because they have not connected in FAITH. These people need someone who does have strong FAITH to connect with God, for them, to agree in prayer with them and give their FAITH a boost.

A FAITH boost happens when two people combine their FAITH in the prayer of agreement. One of them is going to get a boost in their FAITH to receive.

THE FAITH CONNECTION

The Prayer of Agreement, according to John Thomas, is like stringing jumper cables between two batteries. The stronger battery will help, or boost, the weaker battery to start the car that it belongs to. In the Prayer of Agreement, the person with the stronger FAITH will help, or boost the person with weaker FAITH to get their prayers answered, or to get healed, or to receive THE BLESSING.

The stronger battery will not help start the weaker battery's car unless they are **connected** by jumper cables. I cannot help anyone receive from God unless we are united together by the Prayer of Agreement, which is the **connector** between two people.

2 SECRETS TO THE PRAYER OF AGREEMENT

The secrets in order to get results are:

1. When two people unite, or connect together in a prayer of agreement, only **one of them** needs to have FAITH that God **can** and that God **will** answer the prayer, in order to get results.

2. The other person must have FAITH in **the ability** of their PRAYER PARTNER to get the prayer answered.

If your FAITH is not strong enough to connect with God for what you need, connect with someone else and use their FAITH to complete the **FAITH CONNECTION.**

My prayer ministry is based on the Prayer of Agreement and I do have GREAT FAITH to get prayers answered for my Prayer Partners.

HOW TO USE MY FAITH

In order to use MY FAITH to get what you want or need, you must BELIEVE that I can do it. Sometimes I even ask people, "Do you BELIEVE I can do this."

There is no sickness or disease I cannot get healed if a person will just believe I can do it, through the power of God's might, that the Apostle Paul told us to use in Ephesians 6:10.

People call me every day and say, "Pastor Jim, I need to use your FAITH." I say, "OK" and they get healed, receive the BLESSING, or get their prayers answered.

Once people BELIEVE I can get them healed through the power of God's might, I can then use my FAITH in the NAME OF JESUS for their healing.

However, my FAITH will not work for people who are skeptical or do not BELIEVE I can do it. I will not even continue to pray for people who are also having someone else pray for them because I know that they do not have FAITH in **my ability** to get their prayers answered. I do not allow myself to be added to the list of people praying for someone.

When I pray for someone, I mean business and I intend to have it answered. I also do not "Keep people in my prayers." When I pray for someone I mean for that to be the end of it.

Sometimes I will ask people these questions. If Jesus Himself came down here and prayed for you, would you keep looking for someone else to pray for you? Would you fuss and ask a lot of questions and keep begging God to help you, or would you just go home and praise God knowing that your prayer has been answered?

THE RIGHT PRAYER PARTNER

Everyone should have a PRAYER PARTNER. Just make sure that you pick a person who has strong enough FAITH to help get your prayers answered.

I always make my FAITH available to the people in my church and my Prayer Partners. I would think that there must be other ministers who do the same thing.

You cannot use another person's FAITH unless you actually BELIEVE their FAITH will cause you to receive from God. If my PRAYER PARTNERS have FAITH in **my ability** to get their prayers answered, and many do, they will receive every time.

I require all of my PRAYER PARTNERS to watch my 15-minute videos every day to increase their FAITH and strengthen their spirits. That makes it much easier for me to get them healed, BLESSED, and to get their prayers answered for them.

There is nothing wrong with getting help if you know your FAITH is not where it needs to be. I still do that when I need to. When I need something, I will only ask someone to pray for me who I know has the FAITH to get my prayer answered.

I do not have FAITH in the words or prayers of just anyone. However, I can tell you that when Kenneth Copeland spoke THE BLESSING over me I BELIEVED it with all my heart, so much so in fact that I actually felt THE BLESSING come upon me. Our finances have increased in leaps and bounds since that day. That happened because I have FAITH in Brother Copeland's **ability** to speak THE BLESSING over me and in his FAITH.

I would never ask anyone to pray for me, speak healing, or THE BLESSING over me, unless I know they have GREAT FAITH in the Name of Jesus, and I have FAITH in **their ability** to get results. I would never look for just anyone to pray for me or with me. I would look for someone who can actually get my prayers answered!

People who know a lot more about the Bible than I do can argue about this all they want, but the truth of the matter is, I have gotten thousands of people healed and thousands of prayers answered for people who had very little or no FAITH at all. Some were not even saved. My Prayer Partners will tell you that when I combine my FAITH with theirs, in the prayer of agreement, we get amazing results.

When our church was small we went through a period of time in which absolutely everyone who had me pray for them, received an answer. I even told them, "Be careful what you ask for because you are going to get it."

If your FAITH is not where it needs to be in order to receive what you want or need from God, find a Prayer Partner who has GREAT FAITH, to agree with you in prayer and use their FAITH to get what you need. Your first choice should be your Pastor, if he is available.

PEOPLE NEED HELP WITH THEIR FAITH

The reason people like Oral Roberts and the rest of the healing evangelists went around healing sick people was because people **needed help with their FAITH** to get healed. The same is true today. If people could get healed on their own they would not need anyone to pray or speak healing over them. To pray for, or to minister healing to a sick person is actually a prayer of agreement. Healing Evangelist A. A. Allen, spoke often about the prayer of agreement in his meetings.

HANNAH'S PRAYER PARTNER

1 Samuel 1:17, Hannah was praying for a baby when she was beyond the age of conceiving, and Eli the Priest, said to her, "Go in peace and the God of Israel grant thy petition that you have asked of Him."

That was a prayer of agreement! Hannah had FAITH that Eli, could make it happen for her. Eli had FAITH in **his ability** to make it happen, to get her prayer answered through the power of God. Very soon after that, she conceived, had a son and named him Samuel. Because she had FAITH in **the ability** of her Priest to get her prayer answered, she was expecting a baby even before she conceived. **Hannah's PRAYER PARTNER was Eli, her Priest.**

Hannah was not connecting in FAITH herself, or she would have had the request granted on her own. She became connected to Eli, who did connect to God in FAITH by BELIEVING that **God was able** and EXPECTING that **God would** answer Hannah's prayer request.

In the prayer of agreement, the person doing the BELEIVING must BELIVE that **God is able** and also EXPECT that **God will** grant the prayer. The other person must have FAITH in their Prayer Partner's **ability** to get the prayer answered. This combination will get results every time.

HOW JESUS HEALED PEOPLE

When Jesus said to people "Your FAITH has healed you, or your FAITH has made you whole" what exactly did He mean? Was He saying they had FAITH that God would heal them? If that was the case, then why would they even need Jesus? No, their FAITH was based upon the fact that they had **heard** Jesus was healing people, or they had seen Him doing it. They knew that if they could just get to Him, He **could** heal them. When Jesus told people "Your FAITH has made you whole" He was referring to their FAITH in Him, in **His ability** to heal them.

Everyone Jesus healed, agreed with Him for their Healing. They had FAITH in Him and He most certainly had FAITH to heal them. Go through the miracles of Jesus in the Gospels and you will see a common denominator among the people Jesus healed. They had FAITH in Him, in **His ability**, in the Words He spoke, in some cases, His Hands, or even the Hem of His Garment. People had FAITH that Jesus could heal them and **Jesus had FAITH that He could heal them**.

FAITH IN THE ABILITY OF JESUS

Everyone who came to Jesus for healing, BELIEVED that He had the **ability** to heal them.

> **Mark 1:40 a leper came to Jesus, calling out to Him, knelt down to Him, and said, "If you want to, you are able to make me clean." Jesus moved with compassion, touched the man and said, "I do want to, be healed."**

This man **did not have FAITH** that Jesus **would** heal him, but he **did have FAITH** that Jesus **was able** to heal him, if only He wanted to.

Jesus even asked the two blind men in **Matthew 9:27 "Do you BELIEVE I am able to do this? They said, "Yes Lord."** Jesus then used His FAITH to heal them. Once they professed their FAITH in **the ability** of Jesus to heal them, He healed them.

It seems that all the FAITH Jesus needed from people, was for them to have FAITH in **His ability** to heal them. He then used His FAITH to heal them.

> **Mark 5:23 Jairus said to Jesus "My little daughter lies at the point of death: please come and lay Your Hands on her that she may be healed and she will live."**

His FAITH was in **the ability** of Jesus to lay His hands on his daughter and heal her.

I don't know that Jairus was 100% sure that Jesus was going to go with Him and heal his daughter because there was a huge crowd of people around Him. However, I am sure that Jairus was **fully persuaded** that **if Jesus did come** to his house and lay His hands on the little girl, she would be healed and not die.

> **Matthew 8:8 The centurion said to Jesus, "just say the word ONLY" and my servant will be healed."**

He had GREAT FAITH in **the ability** of Jesus, to just speak the Word, and that alone would heal his servant. He had GREAT FAITH in Jesus' Words!

> **Mark 5:25-34 There was a woman who had an issue of blood for twelve years. She heard about Jesus and went to see Him. Because of the crowd she could not get to Him so she said, "If I can just touch His clothes I will be healed.**

The woman's FAITH was in Jesus and she even BELIEVED that touching His garment would heal her, **if** she could just get close enough to touch His garment. She used her FAITH to draw the healing power out of Jesus, through the Hem of His garment.

FAITH IN YOUR ABILITY

People had FAITH in Jesus, BELIEVING that Jesus **could** heal them. The people who got close to Him did indeed receive their healing. It was Jesus using HIS FAITH to heal the people and the people using THEIR FAITH to BELIEVE He could do it. **Jesus had FAITH in His ability to heal people and to perform miracles.** I also have FAITH in my ability to heal people through the Power of God and by the NAME OF JESUS, because Jesus said I can do what He did. (John 14:12)

In 1946 T. L. Osborn went to a William Branham meeting and watched him heal a deaf child, using THE NAME OF JESUS. He said, "I can do that." He started that weekend and had he a great healing ministry all over the world. Oral Roberts watched William Branham and decided he could do the same thing. A. A. Allen watched Oral Roberts heal people and said "I can do that." Then he went around with his huge tent and healed people all over America.

Years ago, we used to go to a friend's house in Tomahawk, Wisconsin and watch Benny Hinn on satellite TV. There was always a large group of people there watching and cheering when people got healed. I would always say to myself, "I am doing that." I was actually doing the same thing, on a one to one basis routinely, while I was at work.

I have FAITH in **my ability** to heal people, BLESS people, and to get prayers answered for people by using THE NAME OF JESUS, Mark 16:17 and the power of God's might, Ephesians 6:10.

Three weeks after I was saved, I was sitting at a used car lot in Tomahawk, Wisconsin, reading Mark 16:17-20. I said, "I am one of them that BELIEVES, **I can do that.**" That same afternoon, an unsaved man with a severely injured knee was completely healed. I asked him, "Do you BELIEVE God can heal your knee?" He said, "Yes" and he was healed.

I have been getting sick and injured people healed ever since that day. Many dying people have been healed. Some were so close to death that they were gasping for breath. One man had been taken off food and water by hospice, to quicken his death. When we got there, I said to him, "What do you want from me?" He whispered, "I want to live." He was completely healed, simply because he told his daughter to call and ask me to come. He knew I could get him healed through the power of God.

Another lady was dying of pancreatic cancer and her family called and asked me to come right away. We were there in ten minutes. She was all yellow, even her eyes. I asked her, "What do you want?" Gasping for each breath, she whispered, "I just want to be comfortable because I am in so much pain." She knew I could make her pain go away through the Name of Jesus. She was made comfortable by being completely healed. Two weeks later the doctors said there was no trace of cancer in her body.

Miracles started happening three weeks after I got saved. I did not question God's Word. I just BELIEVED God's Word and EXPECTED things to happen when I used the Name of Jesus, exactly the way He said in Mark 16:17. And it did and does! People from our town would stop by my office in the morning on their way to work if they were sick. They knew I could get them healed.

I have GREAT FAITH in THE Power that is in THE NAME OF JESUS. I also have GREAT FAITH in **my ability** to use HIS NAME to get people healed and BLESSED. A few years ago, the Lord spoke to me in an audible voice and asked, "What's the difference if there is one person in front of you, or a thousand people?" I replied, "No difference Lord."

I am so confident in **my ability** to get people healed, by the NAME OF JESUS and through the Power of God's Might, that I tell people, if I get to you before you die of sickness or disease, you will not die. That is why people call me from all over the world when they are sick. People have even bought me airplane tickets to come to them when they were sick, including the Pastor of a large church with cancer that had spread to his bones. He was healed.

I BELIEVE with all my heart, that no sickness, disease, generational curse of sickness or poverty, spirit of infirmity, or spirit of death can stand up to **THE POWER** that is **IN THE NAME OF JESUS.** When I use that NAME, I intend to get results and I do.

THE NECESSARY COMBINATION

In order to perform miracles and heal the sick:

- You must have **FAITH in THE NAME OF JESUS**

- You must have **FAITH in your own ability** to do it.

- The person receiving the miracle must BELIEVE that **you have the ability** to do it.

Years ago, on a Wednesday morning, a young man came into my office wearing a back brace and walking very slowly with a cane. I said, "What happened to you?" He replied, "I was lifting an ice fishing shack and blew out two discs in my back." I told him that if he came to our church that evening we would pray for him and he would be healed. He said, "I hope so." I said, "No, if you come out there tonight, God is going to heal you." I will never forget the way he looked at me and then he said, "OK."

That evening he drove 25 miles in an old beat up car, with his wife and three small children, with the temperature at -23 degrees, to get to our church. After the teaching, the person leading the service that night, Neal Syvertson, commanded his back to be healed in the Name of Jesus, while the rest of us stood behind him. 30 minutes later this man, who was not even saved yet, stood up perfectly healed.

It took me over 25 years to fully understand what had happened that night. We all knew that man did not have FAITH to be healed, but he most certainly had received his healing.

That man's FAITH was in the words I spoke to him. He BELIEVED me when I said that we would pray for him and God was going to heal him. Neal, who absolutely BELIEVES that he has **the ability** to get anyone healed of anything, at any time, then used his FAITH in THE NAME OF JESUS to actually heal the man. The necessary combination.

Six months later we received a call from the same man's wife. He had suffered a massive heart attack and she ask us to come to the hospital right away. The nurse told us his heart was severely damaged. He was in the cardiac ICU and was scheduled to be transferred the next morning to a heart center for what they hoped was lifesaving surgery.

They told us he was not allowed any visitors. I said to Mary, "I can get him healed if I can just get in there." I said, "Angels, get us in there." Two minutes later a nurse took Mary and I into his room. The power of God was so strong that one of the nurses almost fell over. He looked at me through all the tubes and his eyes got really big. I put my hand over his chest and said, "IN THE NAME OF JESUS, I command a new heart to be in your chest right now." They made us leave right away.

The next morning, they transferred him to the heart center where they ran a battery of tests and determined that his heart was perfect. That evening he was home playing softball with his team. He said later, "I knew I was going to get healed when you walked into the room." He had FAITH that I could get him healed and I had FAITH in **my ability** to do it in THE NAME OF JESUS. Again, the necessary combination.

Tell people you know who are sick that if they call me, come to one of my meetings, or come to our church, God will heal them. If they do call or come, they will get healed.

I BELIEVE that once a person calls me, or comes to our church, their healing, needs, or BLESSING becomes my responsibility and I take that very seriously.

A man from our church was browsing in the local Christian bookstore. He met a man who told him he had liver cancer and there was nothing more the doctors could do for him. He told the man to come to our church where he would be prayed for and God would heal him. He came and was completely healed.

Another man from our church worked with a young woman who told him she had a melanoma on her leg. The doctors said it had spread. The member of our church said to her, "Follow me, we will go to Pastor Jim's house, he will pray for you and God will heal you." He called me and I said, "Come right over." They came and I told that cancer to leave her in the Name of Jesus. She went back to the doctor several days later for a scheduled biopsy, and the melanoma was totally gone.

A man who attended our church was diagnosed with a melanoma lump on his leg that had spread. He was scheduled for a biopsy. He came to church and I cursed that cancer and told the cancer cells to die. They did the biopsy and found cancer all right, but the cells were all dead. Within a week the lump on his leg was gone.

Two years later, after not seeing this same man and his family for a long while, he, his entire family and friends showed up at church on a Sunday morning. His son's girlfriend, the mother of his children, was brain dead at the hospital. They wanted her back. I commanded her brain to start working in THE NAME OF JESUS. They went to the hospital after church and her brain was starting to have some activity. Two days later she went home completely healed.

A woman full of cancer and down to less than 60 pounds was brought to our church, by her physical therapist. She was totally healed.

A man who had read my book "THE BLESSING" was dying of cancer and he said, "I am going to find Pastor Jim." By the time he found me he could not even walk. His family carried him through the door on a Wednesday evening and he was completely healed.

A young boy was in an ICU unit, dying of a continuous epileptic seizure that the doctors could not stop. Someone from our church contacted his father on Facebook, **told him to contact me and his son would be healed.** He sent me a text and told me the situation. He said, "Its like he has a demon in his head." I told him to call me when he was in the ICU room with his son. The whole family had gathered there and the father called and put me on speaker. I told the demon to leave and the boy was healed instantly. Two days later his father sent me a photo of his son eating at a restaurant with his family.

We had a completely blind woman come to one of our events, EXPECTING to be healed. I knew I could get her healed. I even asked the audience, "Who wants to see a miracle?" In about two minutes she could see perfectly.

When people hear and BELIEVE that they can get healed through me by the power of God, then come to my church, or call me, they will get healed every time. Or, if they BELIEVE that they can get their prayers answered through me by the power of God, that will also happen every time.

There are exceptions to this as we find in Acts Chapter 3. That man at the gate had NO FAITH that Peter could get him healed, yet he still got healed, because Peter BELIEVED he could heal the man through the NAME OF JESUS. We have also had exceptions to this, but as far as I know, most of the people who were brought to me by someone, were told that they were going to get healed. Other people who got healed were just told to call me for healing or to come to our church.

THE HEALING EVANGELISTS

It worked the same way in the meetings of the healing evangelists, during the healing revival, which lasted from 1947 through 1958. When people heard that one of the healing evangelists was coming to town they would stand in line for hours just to get in. Then they prayed that the card they filled out would be drawn. These people went there EXPECTING the evangelist to get them healed. This is the same way people who went to see Jesus were expecting to be healed, if only they could get close to Him.

All of the people who were healed in those meetings had one thing in common, FAITH in **the ability** of the evangelist to get them healed through the power of God. All of the healing evangelists had two things in common, FAITH in THE NAME OF JESUS and FAITH in their **own ability** to get anyone healed of any sickness or disease. The necessary combination.

Oral Roberts would sit in a chair and the sick people would walk past him. The people had FAITH in **his ability** to get them healed through the power of God. He had FAITH in THE NAME OF JESUS, and FAITH in his **own ability** to get them healed, which is the **necessary combination** for the prayer of agreement to work. He would touch them, speak over them in the Name of Jesus and thousands were healed.

A.A. Allen always talked about the prayer of agreement and Mark 16:17. He actually knew how this worked. People had FAITH that he could get them healed through the power of God. He had FAITH in **his ability** and FAITH in THE NAME OF JESUS.

When Brother Hagin would say, "Form a line at the front of the church," people who had needs would run down because they knew that this was their chance to receive from the man of God. Their FAITH was in **the ability** of Brother Hagin to make it happen for them. He certainly had FAITH in **his ability** to heal people, and He had GREAT FAITH in the NAME OF JESUS. The necessary combination.

If you have needs, find someone who has FAITH in **their ability** that they can make it happen for you, and who also has FAITH in THE NAME OF JESUS, and you will get your needs met every single time.

FAITH
FOR SALVATION

FAITH FACT: God does not pick out people to save.

FAITH FACT: You must be born again to be saved and to spend eternity with Jesus in Heaven.

People who die without being born again, by repenting of their sins and receiving Jesus as their Savior, will be lost forever.

Millions of people have MENTAL FAITH in God and in Jesus and sit in church every Sunday morning, but have not received Jesus into their heart and so they are what we call lost.

JESUS MUST KNOW YOU

Millions of people the world over know about Jesus. The question is, does Jesus know you? Do you have a personal day by day walking talking relationship with Him? It is one thing to know about Jesus and quite another to be born again, by receiving Him into your heart as your Savior. The people who are not born again will someday hear Jesus say, "Depart from Me, I never knew you."

When Jesus in in a person's heart they will talk about Him because He is their favorite topic of conservation. When I got born again all I wanted to hear about was Jesus. When we went to some-one's home or a party, I only want to be around people who were talking about Jesus.

The most important thing is to have FAITH for salvation.

All of God's people know that nothing is more important than being born again.

FAITH IN JESUS FOR SALVATION

You must repent of your sins, have FAITH in Jesus as your Savior, give yourself to Him completely and receive Him into your heart to be saved. While the FAITH of someone else can help you with healing, THE BLESSING or getting your prayers answered, salvation is totally up to each person individually.

> **Ephesians 2:8 For by grace are you saved through FAITH; and not because of anything you have done yourself, it is the gift of God.**

There is nothing you can do to earn your salvation. All you need to do is receive it by FAITH.

> **Romans 10:9-10 For if you confess the Lord Jesus and BELIEVE that God raised Him from the dead you shall be saved. BELIEVING in your heart makes you the righteousness of God and with your mouth confession brings salvation.**

Romans 10:13-14, 17 Whoever calls upon the Name of The Lord shall be saved.

This means absolutely anyone can be saved. **14 How can they call if they do not BELIEVE?** They must have FAITH before they call. **How can they BELIEVE unless they have heard of Jesus?** No one can BELIEVE in Jesus without first hearing about Him. **How can they hear without a preacher?** Someone has to tell them about Jesus. **17 So then Faith comes by hearing the Word of God in your ear.**

If you have never received Jesus as your Savior, just pray this prayer, BELIEVE in your heart, and you will be saved.

Heavenly Father, I repent for all of my sins. I believe Jesus is the Son of God and He rose from the dead after suffering for my sins. Lord Jesus, please come into my heart, be my Savior and I will serve You for all of eternity. Amen.

If you just prayed this prayer you will spend eternity in Heaven with Jesus.

ABOUT THE AUTHOR

Pastor Jim Kibler was born in Pittsburgh and grew up in Slippery Rock, Pennsylvania. He is a graduate of Mount St. Mary's College in Emmitsburg, Maryland, and Rhema Bible College in Tulsa, Oklahoma. He also did graduate work in business at George Washington University in Washington, DC.

Pastor Jim and his wife Mary, who is also a graduate of Rhema Bible College, Pastor Life Church in Indialantic, Florida.

Pastor Jim's popular website is www.increasenow.com, a **FREE SITE**, where people around the world watch his FREE 15 Minute videos every day. He teaches about God's Goodness, Healing, Redemption, Abundance and The Blessing.

Also watch Pastor Jim's live broadcast every day by downloading the free **Periscope App** on your phone and follow Pastor Jim Kibler.

FOLLOW PASTOR JIM KIBLER ON FACEBOOK AND INSTAGRAM

In addition, Pastor Jim is a Very Entertaining Conference Speaker and everywhere he speaks, people get healed, finances increase and churches grow. He makes God's Word very easy to understand. He also has a very anointed healing ministry with people being healed of every type of disease and blind eyes opened.

Pastor Jim has a wonderful Prayer Ministry with Prayer Partners all over the world and makes himself available to pray with people who do not have a Pastor to pray with them. He is Personal Pastor to many people who otherwise do not have a Pastor to Talk to, Speak THE BLESSING over them, or Pray the Prayer of Faith for their needs.

His Prayer Ministry has had incredible results. Many people are healed right over the phone, have the curse of the law and generational curses broken and have THE BLESSING activated in their lives.

Pastor Jim's phone number is available at

www.increasenow.com

He is called the **"How To Preacher"** because he not only teaches people what God has promised, but how to receive it.

Other Books by Pastor Jim:

"The Power Of Positive Words"

"How To Pray"

"The Blessing"

"Jesus"

"The Blessing and The Tithe"

"If the Bible Is True"

Made in the USA
Columbia, SC
17 December 2018